Percy Thrower's Step by Step Gardening

Percy Thrower's Step by Step Gardening

Hamlyn
London · New York
Sydney · Toronto

Contents

First published in 1974 by
The Hamlyn Publishing Group Limited
London · New York · Sydney · Toronto
Astronaut House, Feltham, Middlesex,
England
© Percy Thrower and
The Hamlyn Publishing Group, 1974
ISBN 0 600 30072 X
Printed in England by
Cox & Wyman Limited,
London, Fakenham and Reading
Filmset in England by
Tradespools Ltd., Frome, Somerset

ACKNOWLEDGEMENTS
We are grateful to Bradley-Nicholson
Limited for lending the colour illustration
reproduced on page 121. We would also
like to thank the following for providing
the photographs used in this book:
Amateur Gardening, Pat Brindley,
Country Life, Robert Corbin, John
Cowley, Ernest Crowson, Ray Hanson,
Arthur Hellyer, Humex Limited,
A. J. Huxley, Elsa Megson, Robert
Pearson and Harry Smith.

Introduction

Never before has there been such interest in gardening. Never before have so many people been avid for information on every conceivable aspect of this best of all pastimes.

Step by Step Gardening, the natural successor to my *Picture Book of Gardening*, now out of print, is an attempt to provide a visual guide to all that is best in modern gardening, from garden making onwards.

One thing I'm convinced of is that when it is a question of describing practical gardening operations pictures can often tell a story more explicitly, and have more real value, than any number of words. What I have done is to group together a very large number of 'working' pictures – over 550 of them – covering main-line interests and some others as well. These pictures and the text which accompanies them are an indication of the way you, too, can acquire skills which people like myself have picked up over many years.

In addition to ornamental gardening, which must be the pre-occupation of all of us seeking to improve our home environment, I have taken full account of the great interest nowadays in vegetable and fruit growing. It is surprising how much produce can be harvested from quite a small plot if the ground allocated for such purposes is used to best advantage and of course vegetable and fruit cultivation is full of interest for the home owner prepared to give the time to it.

Then there is greenhouse gardening which has so much to offer the enterprising gardener, whether or not he makes do with a cool – or even, maybe, an unheated greenhouse – or is able to maintain reasonably high temperatures and so greatly increase the scope of his activities. What I have done here is to concentrate on the basic skills which need to be developed, if you are to make the most of what you have got.

If this highly illustrated practical guide makes some aspects of gardening easier for you to understand I shall be well pleased.

Percy Thrower

Garden Making

Good planning and preparation are essential to the success of any garden and it is very important not to rush the fundamentals. Top priority must be given to making the garden suit the site. Get to know the nature of your soil and the aspect of your garden then choose those plants which are known to thrive under your conditions. If you are new to the district, talk to more experienced gardening neighbours for their knowledge of the area will be very useful.

Design your garden to fit the architecture of the house and to blend in well with the surroundings. Wherever possible I would favour an informal plan using climbing plants to take away from the starkness of house walls. If your garden is on a slope make a feature of this by gently contouring it, as I have in my garden, or by creating a terraced garden.

The requirements of the other members of the household must be considered and areas for drying clothes and for playing games should be incorporated if these are needed. If you have a limited amount of time to work in the garden, choose plants and features which need a minimum of attention. Roses, ornamental trees and shrubs, herbaceous perennials, which are sturdy enough not to need staking, and naturalized bulbs are all splendid plants for the busy gardener. A paved area or patio, close to the house, is easy to maintain. Keep the garden simple with a few rather than numerous features but try to introduce just that element of surprise to make it interesting.

The kitchen garden is an essential feature of all but the smallest gardens these days and this can be screened off from the rest of the garden with an ornamental hedge or a row of trained fruit trees. When you are taking over an existing garden, which may have been neglected, watch it for a season and find out exactly what it contains, then very gradually adapt it to suit your own plans. Do not make drastic renovations unless these are absolutely necessary and then only after careful thought.

With a new garden plan its full development over a few years and always buy first-class plants from good nurseries.

Making a start When you are in the position of having to build a garden on a new site, or to do a major conversion on an existing garden, the first stage is to prepare a rough sketch plan. The one shown here [1] was prepared for my garden some ten years ago. I do want to stress that it does not have to be beautifully drawn but only needs to be a guide to go by. The important thing is to show the north and south aspects, positions of the house, drive, paths, terrace, and any other main features such as a pool. In my own garden, some of the features were altered as we went along. The final plan, which was drawn a year ago, is also shown [2] and you can see that certain alterations to shapes and sizes of beds etc. have been made.

Soil testing At the same time as you make your garden plan, it is a good idea to test the soil to find out whether it is acid or alkaline. Fairly inexpensive soil-testing kits [3] are available from most garden centres and garden sundries stores. These are simple to use and will tell you how much free lime there is in the soil – this is often expressed as the pH value. pH 7 is neutral being neither acid nor alkaline. Numbers below 7 indicate increasing degrees of acidity. Numbers above 7 indicate degrees of

alkalinity. Plants vary in their preferences for the different sorts of soil, some need an acid soil while others require the presence of lime. The soil in my garden gave a pH value of 6·5 so I realized that by adding peat, which is an acid substance, I could grow azaleas, rhododendrons, camellias, ericas and magnolias. But if the pH is above 7·5, it is advisable not to attempt to grow lime-hating plants and I would like to emphasize here that it is better to grow those plants which suit your soil rather than doing things the other way round and trying to alter the soil to suit the plants' requirements.

Clearing the site Clearing weeds from the garden site is a tedious job which can be made much easier by using a weedkiller. This can be applied most economically from a watering-can fitted with a dribble bar [4]. Paraquat and diquat are especially useful chemicals as they will kill the green parts of any plants with which they come in contact but become inactive on touching the soil. They will not harm brown or woody stems. On bracken and bramble it will be necessary to use a brushwood killer and there are selective weedkillers for use on docks and other deep-rooted weeds. In an area where there is a lot of scrub it is

possible to apply the weedkiller as a fine spray, but it is most important to make sure that there is nothing which will be hurt by drift and for this reason I advise you to use garden chemicals on a still day.

Paths When constructing the garden the position of the paths is very important to the overall garden plan. Any part of the garden which requires frequent visiting in winter demands a path and I feel strongly that there should be paths to all the doors and round the house under the windows to make window cleaning easier. The paths can be made from stone, brick, asphalt, concrete or ashes but all should be laid on a good layer of clinkers or hard rubble. If the surface is to be made of concrete this should be spread over the rubble to a depth of at least 2in. The sides can be formed by laying the concrete between shuttering made from planks placed on their edges [5]. Concrete should be laid in sections of not more than 8ft. in length to allow for expansion and contraction [6]. Check the levels with a square-edged plank. For brick and paving stone paths put a layer of mortar over the rubble and lay the stones on this. It is important that paving is laid absolutely flat and that each brick or stone is firmly embedded.

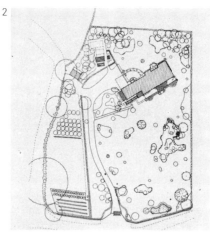

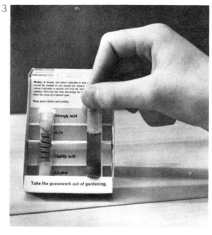

Drainage At an early stage in garden construction it is essential to determine if the natural drainage is sufficient to cope with all types of weather. For example, if you see water standing in parts of the garden, particularly during winter, it may well mean that some additional drainage is necessary. To check whether this is the case dig some 2 to 3-ft. deep test holes and if these remain filled with water for any length of time then it is an indication that some form of drainage must be carried out.

The best and most efficient method of improving drainage is by using land-drain pipes. These can be laid in trenches, 18 in. to 2 ft. deep [1], which are usually arranged in a herringbone pattern made up of side drains running into the main drain [2]. The pipes used in the main drain must have a larger diameter than those in the side drains. The whole system should lead to the lowest point in the garden. It is, of course, necessary to employ some means of getting the water away.

The usual method is to dig a deep pit or soakaway at the lowest point in the garden [3] and to run the main drain into this. The pit should be filled with broken brick or rubble [4] and the surplus water will eventually drain through. This works

well when the subsoil is of sand or gravel but if the soil is clay it is not always so easy to get the water away from the soakaway. In a case like this it is better to try and run the main drain into a ditch but whatever you do take care not to run the surplus water on to your neighbour's garden. The drain pipes in the trenches should be covered with rubble, clinker or stones before the soil is replaced. In cultivated areas there should be a depth of 10 to 12 in. of soil above the rubble, in grassed areas a depth of 6 to 8 in. will be sufficient.

Another system of drainage which is quite effective and rather cheaper and quicker is the simple clinker drain. This is prepared in much the same way as the drain-pipe system, digging $1\frac{1}{2}$ to 2 ft. deep trenches which should be filled to a depth of 12 in. with a layer of rubble [5,6] and then filled with soil to surface level. The main drain is run into a soakaway.

The soils which tend to be poorly drained are the heavier clay types which are made up of very small soil particles that pack closely together and hold moisture readily. However, they may not be bad enough to need a major drainage system and can be greatly improved by good cultivation.

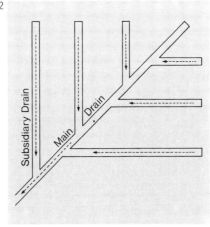

Soil cultivation No soil is ideal for every purpose and most of us will have to cope with a soil which is either too light and free draining or too heavy and inclined to be waterlogged. The best way of overcoming these tendencies is by good cultivation – digging in plenty of organic matter to improve texture.

I like to get the job of digging done in the autumn, as early as possible before the soil gets too wet. Then the soil can be left in rough clods to be broken down by the alternating frosts, rain and snow of winter. Do not underestimate how much the weather can help, particularly with heavy clay soils. Before digging, remove any debris from the surface [1] and kill as many weeds as possible by using a weedkiller. Remove all roots of perennial weeds as you dig. The actual digging can be done in a number of ways and if there is much ground involved then I recommend the use of a rotary cultivator. This makes the job much easier and leaves the soil in an ideal condition [2]. These machines can be hired or you can get a gardening contractor to do the job for you. If organic matter is to be incorporated, spread it on the surface and turn it under during the digging process. When digging with a spade always dig to the

full depth of the blade throwing the soil forward to form a trench which can be used for the incorporation of any peat or compost [3]. If you have heavy clay soil then forking over the bottom of the trench improves drainage.

Garden compost Large quantities of organic matter are used in improving soil texture and, as farmyard manure is often difficult to come by, it is important to save all waste green material for composting. Almost anything which will decay quickly can be used for this purpose: grass clippings, leaves, hedge clippings, faded flowers, vegetable and fruit refuse from the kitchen. Never use diseased growth, weeds which have gone to seed, the roots of the perennial weeds such as bindweed or couch grass or any heavy woody growth.

The heap should be built to a height and width of about 3 ft. and I like to use the plastic-covered netting bins [4] to keep it tidy. To encourage and increase the rate of decay use an accelerator, such as sulphate of ammonia, Nitro-chalk or one of the proprietary products made for this purpose and sprinkle this over each 9-in. layer of refuse [5]. If sulphate of ammonia is used then it should be alternated between the layers with hydrated lime. As the heap is built,

sprinkle frequently with water any material which appears dry.

After about four weeks, turn the heap bringing the inside portions to the outside and watering any dry parts.

Chemical fertilizers Apart from the compost and other organic matter plants need a number of chemical substances to complete their growth, flowering and fruiting satisfactorily but from a practical viewpoint only four need be considered. The others are usually present in most soils, particularly those which are well supplied with organic matter. These four important substances are: nitrogen, which increases the length of stem and size of leaves; potash, which increases the depth of colour in leaves and flowers and acts as a general stimulant; phosphorus, which encourages the growth of roots, flowers and fruits and lime, which helps to correct soil acidity and improves the texture of heavy soils. It is important to apply a balanced amount of these chemicals and for most purposes I choose a general fertilizer.

On heavy soils I usually apply fertilizers in the autumn [6] but on light soils it is better to wait until spring. The best time to apply lime is during the autumn and winter and at least a month after any organic matter is added.

Paving This can be used in a number of interesting ways in the garden: to provide a terrace by the house, as a surround to the pool, to make a patio garden or simply as an ornamental feature. There is a wide range of paving stones in a selection of colours and shapes and such an area can be made most attractive. However, when considering the colours of the stone I always avoid the use of too much colour, some of the softer shades can be attractive but I feel that the colour in the garden should come from the flowers and foliage and not from walls, ornaments or paving. In fact, when laying areas of paving I like to see spaces left for low-growing plants [1] such as the thymes, dianthus, saxifrages, sedums and small hypericums. On larger areas the use of individual small shrubs will break the flatness and relieve any monotony. When using stone, and particularly concrete, you have got to include plants to soften the effect and help it to blend in with the rest of the garden.

Stones can be used to make interesting ornamental features. Here [2], I am using broken paving to make the surround for a statue, though it might equally well hold a sundial. The spaces are left for small rock plants.

Another idea which I like for breaking the flatness of an area of paving is also illustrated here [3]. One of the paving stones is left out at intervals and the area involved filled with rows of pebbles or cobblestones embedded in mortar. Use a board [4] to make sure that all the pebbles are laid to an even height and that none come above the level of the surrounding paving.

Screening Screens are ideal for use in the small garden or on the terrace to provide shelter and extra privacy. For this purpose I particularly like the pre-cast pierced concrete blocks [5] which are available in a large variety of patterns. When erecting them, always use a spirit level to check the level of the blocks as they are laid [6]. Such screens can also be made of brick or wood either in the form of open slat or ranch type fencing or the interwoven [7] or lapped fencing which provides a solid surface.

Any form of fencing, and especially the solid kinds, must be planted with climbers to be really effective.

Steps When laying steps [8] it is very important to get them correct or stones may come loose and they become dangerous. So if you are not a handyman then bring in someone who knows what he is doing to lay them for you.

Pergola Pergolas are covered walks like a continuous series of arches. To me they always have an old-world charm and can add a great deal of interest as a garden feature or when used to soften the lines of a house that is rather set and square. The uprights may be of wood, brick or concrete blocks, but the cross members are usually made of timber. All the timber used in garden constructions should be treated with a preservative which is harmless to plants. The pergola which I built to soften the lines of my own house and help it blend in with the garden is made from sawn timber and rustic timber [1]. The square oak sawn timber provides the strength while the rustic timber helps to relieve any hardness. When constructing a pergola it is important to make sure that the whole structure is securely anchored by sinking the base of each upright into a piece of drain pipe and wedging it in position [2]. My pergola was constructed over the terrace in front of the house and is seen here [3] soon after its completion and before the climbing plants had grown sufficiently to mask its hard lines. For a list of climbers I grow on it see page 40.

If you do not have room for a pergola then an arch is useful to give height to the garden design and may even be preferable to trees in a small area. It will also provide an opportunity to grow some of the lovely climbers that are available.

Covering up operations There are essential parts of the house construction which are such an eyesore that they cry out for some sort of camouflage and one of the worst offenders is the manhole cover, which can so easily spoil an otherwise attractive area. An easy way round this problem is to plant one of the prostrate conifers at each end so that as they grow the flat branches will cover the ironwork [4]. For this purpose I use *Cotoneaster horizontalis*, *Juniperus sabina tamariscifolia*, *Juniperus pfitzeriana aurea* or *Juniperus horizontalis*.

The fishbone cotoneaster, *C. horizontalis*, is also a good choice for furnishing an expanse of brickwork and for covering a drain [5]. Drain pipes themselves are hardly things of beauty and it is an easy matter to train a climbing plant around them as I am doing with this early dutch honeysuckle [6]. But an important point to remember here is to cut it back when it reaches the top of the pipe so that it does not get underneath the guttering.

Garden equipment Everybody when starting to garden wants to know the essential tools required to work efficiently. To begin with, I would name the spade, fork, rake and hoe; with these it is possible to do most of the cultivating. After this come a trowel, secateurs for pruning [1,2] and shears for grass and hedge cutting. When choosing the tools it really is an investment to buy good ones because with care these will last a life time. Chrome armour and stainless steel tools cost more but they are also easier to use and to keep clean and if you can afford them you will find that in the long run they are the best buy.

Other tools to be acquired gradually include a wheelbarrow, watering-can, hose and lawn mower. Nowadays wheelbarrows are often made of plastic or fibreglass and the lightness of these is a boon for lady gardeners. Lawn mowers are dealt with on page 18.

Of course, there are now a number of powered tools coming on to the market and all are designed to make various aspects of gardening easier. Apart from the powered lawn mowers you will find cultivators [3], lawn edgers and hedge trimmers.

Another important acquisition is a sprayer to control the various pests and diseases which are found in every garden at some time or another. There are so many different kinds available, many made of lightweight plastic materials [4], that it will not be difficult to find the right one for your particular needs. A good pneumatic sprayer with a strong plastic container will be found the most generally useful. Weedkillers are usually best applied from a watering-can fitted with a dribble bar.

I would like to add a word of warning here about the need for using all garden chemicals with great care. Always read the manufacturer's instructions before use and follow them in every detail, store the chemicals out of the reach of children and animals and wash all equipment well after use. I think it is much safer to keep the watering-can used for weedkiller application solely for this purpose and in this way you will not have any accidents.

All the tools should be kept in a dry shed [5] or garage. Wash and dry them after use [6] and rub tools not made of stainless steel with an oily rag as this will help to prevent rusting.

Garden buildings Sheds are rarely ornamental and it is often a problem to position them in a small garden. As far as possible keep them away from the windows of the house and screen them with shrubs or climbing plants. Summer houses are a popular feature but once again these should be positioned with care and well planted with climbers to blend in with the garden. I prefer the idea of having a conservatory or sun lounge built on to the living room (page 120).

The Lawn

The lawn is one of the main features in nearly every garden in the country. Nothing is more pleasing than a smooth expanse of well-kept grass and a good lawn will set the standard for the rest of the garden to follow. Although we cannot all achieve lawns like bowling greens we can go a long way towards that aim by making careful preparations beforehand and by regular maintenance afterwards. There is no need, however, for a lawn to be absolutely level. A sloping lawn, provided the slope is gentle to allow for easy mowing, can be very attractive.

When making a new lawn the first decision must be whether to use seed or turf. I would recommend seeding whenever possible for it is much less expensive than buying turves and the finished lawn is usually better. The preparatory work for both is just the same. If the area to be grassed down is not very large and there are children and animals in the family whom it would be difficult to keep off seeded ground then turfing has obvious advantages. If you decide to convert meadow grass to a lawn or when you have taken over a lawn which has been neglected, a good result will eventually be achieved by regular mowing, general maintenance and treating with a selective weedkiller.

It is often a good plan, when taking over a new garden, to put a good deal of it down to grass. Eventually, when time allows, flower beds can be cut out of the grass and planted up as soon as they have been dug over for, if the lawn has been looked after, they will be virtually free of pernicious weeds.

Many gardeners make themselves a lot of unnecessary work in mowing by having right-angled corners to the lawns and beds of rectangular, circular or oval shape. Much labour can be saved by arranging for all corners to be gently curved and for all beds to be of such a shape that you can mow round them easily without having to stop and back the machine. The simplest shape for this purpose is a long, fish-like shape without the tail fin.

Many people fail to remember that lawn grasses are plants which need feeding and looking after just like other plants. Routine management of a lawn is important and is detailed in the pages which follow.

Seeding There are many different lawn seed mixtures available to suit all purposes. Where the lawn will be subjected to much wear from children and animals, a good hard-wearing mixture containing crested dogstail and other coarser grasses with flat, wide blades should be chosen. This will require less mowing but will need watching to prevent weeds establishing themselves and spreading in the rather open sward. A fine mixture, including fescues and browntop, will produce a closely knit turf consisting mainly of grass with round, wiry blades. Such a lawn will need cutting at least twice a week at the height of the summer but will present a first-class appearance.

The best times for spring sowing are late March and April in the South and April and May in the Midlands and North but the best time of all in the South is August or September as there are unlikely to be periods of prolonged drought just when the young grass is getting established. In the Midlands and North spring sowing is best for the autumn is more likely to be wet and cold and trouble from damping off disease may follow.

The site should be well drained and the soil carefully prepared. For a spring sowing dig the plot over the previous autumn so that the frost and snow can weather the soil and break down the rough clods into a workable tilth. Remove the roots of all the perennial weeds, especially couch grass, as you go along [1]. If you are planning to sow a lawn in the autumn let the ground lie fallow during the summer and hoe it occasionally to break down the lumps and keep the newly germinated weeds under control.

A few weeks before sowing it may be necessary to work coarse sand into the top few inches of a heavy soil as an extra guard against waterlogging. The quantity can be anything up to 14 lb. per sq. yd. A dressing of fibrous peat is useful on any soil, again worked into the top few inches [2]. In this case it is the sandy soils which will require the greater quantities.

Although a very attractive lawn can be made on a gently sloping or contoured site, it is important at this stage to level out any unsightly bumps and depressions so that the finished lawn does not present a lumpy appearance. This can usually be sufficiently accurately measured by the eye.

Seven to ten days before sowing rake the soil down to a fine tilth and remove any large stones [3]. If you spot any leatherjackets, wireworms and like grubs give the soil a dressing of BHC or trichlorphon. Firm the soil by treading so that it is as even as possible [4] and then rake again at right angles to the previous raking. Finally dress with a well-balanced compound fertilizer [5].

Sowing should be done on a fine, still day when the soil is neither very wet nor very dry. For more accurate sowing mark the plot out into yard-wide strips with lengths of string [6]. The rate of sowing is $1\frac{1}{2}$ to 2 oz. per sq. yd. A wheeled distributor can also be used as described on page 20. After sowing rake the soil lightly and carefully over the seed and then string black cotton over the plot if birds are likely to be a nuisance. It is possible to obtain seed treated with bird repellent, and bird repellent sprays are available for spraying the seed before sowing or the ground afterwards.

Turfing The best time of the year to lay turves is between November and April on a dry day when the soil is moist but workable. It is important to buy good quality turves and, if possible, to inspect them before purchasing. Try to avoid turves which have a large proportion of weeds and poor quality grasses. The best turf comes from sea-washed marshes but this is very expensive and often difficult to get established.

Turves are cut in rectangular pieces of 3 ft. by 1 ft. and are 1½ in. thick. They are delivered rolled up. If they are not going to be used immediately, they should be unrolled otherwise the grass will turn yellow and will be weak. At this time remove any weeds which are likely to prove troublesome such as dandelions and plantains.

The preparation of the soil is the same as for seeding and the surface should be smooth [1]. Turf is laid so that the rows are bonded like bricks. The first row should be started by laying half a turf and the second with a full turf and so on to achieve this effect. Always work from a board to avoid consolidating the surface soil and ensure that each turf fits closely against its neighbours and on the soil beneath. As the turves are laid they can be lightly beaten down on to the surface of the soil with a smooth wooden block or a spade [2]. After laying dress the cracks with a topdressing of either sand or a mixture of loam and peat or leafmould [3] and brush it well in [4] to encourage the grass to extend fresh roots into the turf next to it and so knit quickly and strongly. Trim the edges with a half moon edging iron [5] or a sharp spade.

No pathway should lead directly on to the lawn unless it is continued in the form of stepping stones sunk to the level of the turf for easy mowing. Where pathways lead on to the lawn you will have worn patches which will look shabby and will constantly need renewing. The stones chosen should be hard, large enough to step on comfortably with flat, level surfaces and an even depth, and should have a pleasing colour and substance. They should be placed on the lawn as they are to be laid and cut around with a half moon edging iron [6]. Each one is then placed to one side and the pattern so formed is cut out to the depth of the stone [7] which is then returned to its position where it should sit firmly [8].

Mowing Mowing – the most important part of lawn maintenance – must be done correctly. The height of the cut is important and the mower should be set accurately [1]. It should not be so low that the grass is shaved to the ground level with the result that brown patches appear and moss and other unwanted plants move in nor should it be so high as to lead to the introduction of the coarser grasses, especially on fine lawns. The average lawn will not want cutting closer than $\frac{3}{8}$ in. and should not be longer than $\frac{5}{8}$ in. The finer lawns require mowing closer than those containing coarser grasses.

During the main growing season, grass should be cut at least once a week and really fine lawns should be mown twice a week. The first cutting may be necessary as early as March and it should not be close. Set the mower at slightly under 1 in. and gradually reduce it as the frequency of cutting increases. Towards the end of the season raise the setting again so that the last cuts leave 1 in. of top growth on the grass. Cutting can be carried out in the winter to keep the grass trim but it should be done on a mild, dry day when the ground is not frosted or waterlogged, again with the mower set at 1 in.

A new lawn from seed should not be cut until it is at least 2 in. high. The blades of the mower must be very sharp so that the young seedlings are not pulled out of the ground and the mower must be set at the maximum height. This is gradually lowered as the grass becomes established. Lawns from turves should be sufficiently well established in two to three weeks for mowing if this is necessary.

A mower is probably the most expensive piece of garden equipment which you are likely to buy so it is essential to look after it. It should be kept as clean and dry as possible and well oiled [2, 3]. The cutting blades should be really sharp (though these should be sharpened professionally) and the various related parts should be kept in working unison with each other. During the winter either overhaul your machine yourself, or, better still, get it serviced. Always store it in a cool dry place.

Your choice of lawn mower will depend on the amount that you can afford to spend and the area of grass to be cut. For very small lawns, of course, a hand-propelled side-wheel or roller-type [4] mower is all that is required but for larger areas a powered mower (electric or petrol-engined) is almost a necessity [5, 6].

Cylinder or reel lawn mowers give a scissors type cut between revolving blades and a fixed bottom blade while rotary grass cutters slash the grass off with the action of a scythe or sickle. Cylinder mowers, which are hand or power driven, give a cleaner, more even finish than rotary mowers which are always power driven.

1

2

3

4

5

6

A well-maintained lawn will set the standard for the rest of the garden to follow and regular management will be rewarded

Feeding Lawn grass, perhaps more than other plants, requires nutrients to keep it vigorous and green because its top growth is constantly being removed. There are plenty of proprietary compound lawn fertilizers available and April is the most valuable time of the year to apply one [1]. A further application at the end of June, watered in if the weather is hot and dry, will keep the grass a good colour for the rest of the summer. At the end of September a further dressing can be given to strengthen the root growth and to enable the grass to withstand the winter cold well. It is best to avoid applying high nitrogenous fertilizers at this time of the year since they will make the grass soft and lush so that it is easily susceptible to the cold and to fungus diseases.

Follow the manufacturer's instructions as to the amount of fertilizer to apply very carefully for an overdose can cause scorching which will make unsightly brown patches on the lawn. Spread it as evenly as possible and you might find it helpful to divide the lawn into square yards or yard-wide strips with string or canes. Fertilizer distributors are available for larger areas [2]. These have rollers calibrated to allow certain quantities of fertilizer to be released as required.

They can also be used for seed sowing.
Topdressing A topdressing of loam, peat and sand (or leafmould, dried sludge or well-rotted farmyard manure, mixed with or substituted for the other ingredients) should be given to the lawn in the spring or autumn. This is to improve the structure of the top few inches of the soil and to prevent it deteriorating or becoming short of humus material. It also provides a good basis for new grass shoots to root into and helps to fill in the minor hollows. It is usual to apply 2 to 3lb. of the mixture per sq. yd. and to work it into the surface with a stiff broom or the back of a rake [3]. It will smother the grass if left on the surface and will do more harm than good.
Watering Watering a lawn is a more exacting task than it might at first seem. The water must be given evenly, slowly and in sufficient quantities to soak down at least 4in. Whilst you must be careful not to overwater, it is more important that you do not underwater. Do not forget that during periods of prolonged drought you may be restricted in applying water to your garden by your local council.

Do not turn the hose on and just leave it to flood the lawn. The water will then run off the sides if the soil is dry or down

the cracks without soaking in first. It will do little more than waterlogging the top inch of the soil. The water is best applied as a spray so that it reaches the grass as would natural rainfall. There are several ways of doing this. A perforated plastic hose, laid straight across the grass, will give a fine spray which is quickly absorbed without flooding [4]. The hose is pierced so that the spray comes out at different angles thus enabling the whole of the area to be covered evenly. There are also oscillating sprinklers and pulsating sprinklers. The former have a fixed central point which turns from side to side to fan out water over a rectangular area from a short tube in the centre supported on a metal stand [5]; the latter water a complete circle or segments of a circle [6].

Aerating The aeration of a lawn is one of the most important jobs in its maintenance. The soil will become more and more compacted due to the pressure of constant mowing and general traffic. There is a resulting loss of air at the roots of the grass which die. On heavy soils the drainage may also be impaired which will make the soil sour and the grass very unhealthy. Spiking – making holes in the turf at regular intervals to a depth of 4in. – should be carried out to overcome these problems.

There are several ways of doing this. An ordinary garden fork can be pushed into the lawn at about 6-in. intervals [1]. There are also foot-operated spikers [2] and a tool which has spikes mounted on a cylinder which can be pushed [3]. Spiked rollers can be fitted to a mower and a special hollow-tined fork is available which removes cores of soil completely and is, therefore, the most efficient way. The holes so made can be filled with sand or a sand and soil mixture. Spiking should be carried out in the autumn and if the weather has been very wet in the spring too.

Raking Raking – to remove dead grass, leaves and decayed vegetation which may be lying on the surface of the soil – should be done in the spring and autumn [4]. A wire-tined rake is best but if the lawn has moss in it do not rake until the moss has been killed for this will only help to spread the moss.

Brushing Brushing, especially before mowing, with a stiff broom will greatly help to improve the condition of the lawn. It, too, will remove any unwanted vegetation and also any stones which may damage the mower.

Edging After mowing, the edges of the lawn can be trimmed with short or preferably long-handled shears [5]. Where the edge has become badly overgrown, a new edge to the lawn can be cut with a really sharp spade or better still with a half moon edging iron [6]. The new edge should be marked with a taut piece of string or a straight-edged plank as a guide for cutting. For a badly worn edge cut a turf containing the worn patch and a fair amount of good grass [7] and simply turn this around so that the worn patch is transferred to the inside of the lawn [8]. This can then be treated with a fertilizer and will soon recover.

Plantings of dwarf conifers can be very attractive especially when those of contrasting foliage colours are grown side by side

Pests The chief pest of lawns is the leatherjacket, the larva of the cranefly or daddy-long-legs. The grey grubs are about one inch long and they inflict damage by feeding on the roots of the grass just below soil level so that the grass dies causing unsightly brown patches. These are especially to be noticed in the early spring. To confirm that any brown patches are due to leatherjackets, flood the area with water [1] and leave overnight covered with sacking [2]. By the morning some of the leatherjackets will have surfaced and can be swept up. BHC applied as a spray or dust to the area will also prove effective.

Moles and worms are only a nuisance if they are present in large numbers. They can both do a lot of good – moles by eating leatherjackets and other grubs and worms by aerating the lawn – but moles make unsightly mounds on the lawn and worms create casts. The moles can be driven out by placing a few lumps of calcium carbide in their runs. Derris will kill worms underground as will chlordane. Mowrah meal can be watered on to the soil under pressure and will act as an expellant driving the worms to the surface. They can then be brushed off.

Diseases It is not necessary to distinguish between the diseases of a lawn – just to

determine whether the reason of any damage is due to a fungus or some other cause. Turf diseases thrive in cold damp conditions and where an excess of nitrogenous fertilizer has been applied too late in the summer, causing soft, disease-prone growth. In wet weather fungus-infected grass tends to become slimy and sometimes fine white or pink threads can be seen in the dying grass. The grass first turns yellow, then brown and affected patches may be small and more or less circular, or much larger and less regular. A well-kept lawn should be free of any disease but calomel dust may be applied to any infected areas.

Weed control In the main lawn weeds fall into two classes – one, the kind of weed with a flat rosette habit of growth which enables it to escape the mower, such as plantains, daisies and to a lesser extent, docks and dandelions, which under lawn conditions tend to grow flat on the ground; the other is the creeping, trailing type of weed, which roots at each leaf joint such as speedwell, mouse-ear chickweed, pearlwort and sea milkwort. This kind of weed often also has very small and sometimes hairy leaves which make it unlikely to absorb sufficient hormone weedkiller at any one time to kill it completely.

If there are only a few weeds on the lawn it may be sufficient to dig these out very carefully with a sharp knife [3] or to treat them with a selective weedkiller, applied either from an aerosol or a puffer pack or with a special tool which injects weedkiller into and on to the leaves of the weed. For bad infestations it will be necessary to treat the whole lawn with a selective weedkiller using as fine a spray as possible [4]. There are several of these weedkillers available sold under various trade names.

A lawn made from seed must not be treated with ordinary selective weedkiller for at least three months after germination and it is also wise to allow the same amount of time to pass before treating a lawn made from turf.

Lawnsand is an old remedy for getting rid of weeds and it is still a good one. It burns the top growth of the weeds turning them black. It may also discolour the grass but this will be only temporary. Best results are obtained if no rain follows its application for 48 hours, after which it should be watered in [5].

While moss may be removed in the first instance by proprietary moss killers [6], it will return to those lawns where the growing conditions are not improved.

Foundation Planting

By the term foundation planting I mean getting in the permanent plants – trees and shrubs – which will form the framework of the garden. I have also included in this chapter a section on that most popular of flowering shrubs – the rose.

Trees and shrubs are invaluable subjects for not only does their beauty enhance the garden, many with more than one season of show, but they are also labour saving for once planted many of them need little attention beyond an annual pruning and some of them do not need even that. The leaves of many shrubs and small trees turn a glorious colour in the autumn and many more have a good crop of berries to follow their flowers so it is possible, even in quite small gardens, to have shrubs of interest all the year round. It is important to create a well-balanced effect by planting a pleasing ratio of evergreens, conifers and deciduous subjects.

Do not plant anything which will take over the garden, screen out the light from the house or choke other plantings. There are prostrate creeping varieties, others which attain a very small height and that very slowly and still more which are upright and narrow in habit. A good nurseryman's catalogue will offer you a wide choice. There are some small trees which make excellent lawn specimens and those chosen for this purpose should have neat, attractive habits. The weeping cherry and weeping birch will look very good planted in a lawn but the weeping willows should be avoided.

Many shrubs are ideal as ground cover plants for clothing banks and for planting under larger specimens. Ground cover plants form a carpet which will to a large extent suppress weeds and make soil cultivation unnecessary. Those used for an underplanting must be tolerant of a certain amount of shade but this is not a necessary attribute for those shrubs used for clothing banks.

Some shrubs and small trees look well near water features and in this connection the willows immediately come to mind and also the coloured-barked dogwoods. Even a rock garden can be planted with a selection of trees and shrubs if miniature forms are chosen.

Planting Deciduous trees and shrubs can be planted at any time between early November and the end of March provided the ground is not frozen or waterlogged. Evergreens, however, are best planted in September and October or during late March, April and May. This is because they are never inactive and it is important for them to make new roots quickly so that the loss of moisture through the leaves is made good before the plant is adversely affected. By planting them at the times recommended the roots should quickly become established for the soil will still be warm in the autumn and in the spring it will be warming up after the winter cold.

Evergreens should be watered freely for the first few weeks after planting and if the weather turns exceptionally warm they should be sprayed occasionally overhead. Conifers, on the other hand, have comparatively narrow and small leaves which do not lose water nearly so rapidly as those of broad-leaved trees and shrubs and they can be planted at the same time as deciduous specimens. They do, however, resent root damage and so should be planted when young or from containers. Container-grown trees and shrubs of whatever nature can be planted at any time of the year and these

are discussed more fully under roses (page 36).

Since trees and shrubs are permanent features in the garden, they should be sited with care. It is important to have an idea of the shrub's overall height and width when it is fully grown so that ample room can be left for its development.

The preparation of a shrub border is similar to that of the site for a hedge and readers should turn to page 42 where more information is given. Here I am planting a specimen shrub – a magnolia – in a lawn. The turf has been removed to one side on to a piece of paper and a planting hole has been dug which will take the roots of the magnolia when they are well spread out and will allow the shrub to be planted to the same depth as it was in the nursery. The old soil mark is usually clearly visible. The soil removed from the planting hole has also been heaped on to a piece of paper. The turf is put into the bottom of the planting hole and is chopped up with a spade [1]. Some well-rotted manure or other similar organic matter is added [2] together with a little peat. The magnolia is taken from the sacking which was protecting its roots and preventing them from drying out and positioned carefully

in the centre of the planting hole with all its roots well spread out around it [3]. It is advisable before planting to cut back any damaged roots to the undamaged parts to prevent the entry of disease.

A strong wooden stake is then firmly secured in the ground so that it is about 2 in. away from the main stem of the magnolia [4]. Be careful when securing the stake not to damage any of the roots. Fine soil is worked around the roots of the shrub [5] and then some of the excavated soil is returned. The planting is finished by adding a layer of peat and by firming [6].

Azaleas and bluebells make excellent companions in a woodland setting. Both flower in May and early June and will tolerate shade

Staking Newly planted trees and shrubs should be firmly secured to their stakes with strong ties. Patent adjustable ties are available [1] but home-made ties can be improvized by using strong tarred twine and old rags, sacking or nylon stockings [2]. The important thing is not to let the tie chafe or strangle the plant and regular inspections should be carried out to make sure that this is not happening.

Protection Sometimes trees and shrubs need protecting against the weather and animals and they are especially vulnerable just after they have been planted and when they are young. Rabbits and hares will gnaw at the tender bark of young trees and if these are likely to be a nuisance, black polythene may be tied around the main stem to deter them [3]. A circle of wire netting may also be erected round the tree.

Newly planted conifers will need protection from drying winds otherwise the tips of their branches may turn brown. A screen made from an old sack will provide good shelter if it is placed on the windward side of the plants to break the force of the wind. This screen should be firmly secured with stakes and should be made slightly higher than the plants [4]. It should be removed in the spring. More temporary protection is afforded by wrapping the plants in clear polythene sheeting on days and nights when very cold or windy weather is forecasted [5].

Sharp frosts can also cause considerable damage during the first winter particularly to those slightly tender shrubs which are planted against a wall for added protection. These are dealt with more fully in the next chapter. Clear polythene sheeting [6] and bags are again invaluable or the shrub may be wrapped around with straw [7].

During the first winter, frosts or strong winds may loosen the plants as they will not have rooted into the soil. Throughout the winter, at regular intervals, I check my newly planted trees and shrubs and refirm them if necessary [8].

Aftercare The critical period for all newly planted trees and shrubs is April, May and June, when there are likely to be dry spells. This is the time when plenty of water should be given for if the plants become dry at the roots for any length of time their growth will be seriously retarded. I spray my new evergreens overhead each dry evening for a few weeks after planting to cut down on the amount of moisture lost through the leaves [1]. The plants can also be wrapped in polythene bags for a few weeks to conserve moisture [2]. This shrub is *Mahonia japonica*.

I find that newly planted trees and shrubs benefit greatly from mulching as this helps to keep moisture in the soil during dry periods. The mulch may be of organic matter – garden compost, farmyard manure, shoddy, spent hops – peat or even grass clippings, provided that the lawn has not been recently treated with a weedkiller and it should be spread around the plants so that it is 3 to 4in. thick [3]. Thereafter I do this every year in the spring for a mulch besides conserving moisture will also suppress weeds and if it is organic in nature it will provide some nutrients. I mulch rhododendrons and azaleas every year with peat or grass clippings because these shrubs like the moist, well-drained conditions which this provides them with [4].

Before applying the annual mulch, I feed all my trees and shrubs with a well-balanced fertilizer applied at the rate recommended by the manufacturer [5]. This dressing can be forked lightly into the top few inches of the soil although forking must be done with care as some trees and shrubs are surface rooting and they could be damaged. However, careful forking to aerate the soil and to remove weeds can be very beneficial.

Weedkillers based on the chemical paraquat may be used around trees and shrubs but must be applied with care for they must not come into contact with the leaves of the trees and shrubs [6]. A watering-can with a dribble bar is the best for a border. These weedkillers act through the chlorophyll in the leaves of the weeds to kill them and they will also kill any other leaves with which they come into contact. All chemicals must be mixed very carefully according to the manufacturer's instructions.

Moving a tree People often ask me about the best way of moving a tree or shrub from one part of the garden to another. This can be difficult to do and it is a job which two people will do much better than one.

Here we are moving a weeping cherry to make a specimen tree on a lawn. The Japanese cherries are my favourite members of the genus *Prunus* and Kiku Shidare Zakura, also known as Cheal's weeping cherry, has deep pink, double flowers on drooping branches. We successfully moved this tree in a few hours. Lifting was done with great care with a spade and finally a fork to tease out as much of the root system as possible [1] and although we had to cut through some of the stronger roots the greater part of the root system was lifted with the tree. We used sacking to carry the tree to its new position to prevent the roots from drying out [2,3]. We had already half prepared the planting hole. Prunus trees have wide spreading root systems and the hole was made larger to accommodate all the roots after the tree had been positioned [4]. The tree was planted to the same depth as it had been in its original position. A stake was firmly secured into the ground [5] and fine soil was worked round the roots and firmed [6]. After planting the edge of the hole was neatened.

Pest and disease control Well-kept trees and shrubs will suffer very little from pests and diseases. It is wise, however, to keep a good lookout for an attack and to take the necessary control measures in the early stages before the pest or disease has become established. Regular spraying with derris or malathion throughout the summer months will keep most of the common pests at bay.

Ornamental trees and shrubs which belong to the genus *Prunus* are subject to three diseases which also attack peaches, plums and cherries. These are bacterial canker, leaf curl and silver leaf which are described in the fruit chapter on pages 88 and 89. This group of trees and shrubs also suffer from gumming which is described on page 86. Leaf spot may be controlled by spraying with Bordeaux mixture or zineb. The fungi which cause mildew thrive in damp conditions. Spray the plants with thiram or dinocap. Rust is controlled by spraying at frequent intervals with zineb or thiram.

The delicate flowers of the hybrid shrub rose Frühlingsmorgen grace the garden in May and
June

Pruning Many gardeners worry too much about the pruning of trees and shrubs considering it to be a complicated task. However, it is really quite simple provided a few basic principles are understood.

First consider the reasons for pruning. These are to encourage the formation of flowers and, in some cases, fruits and to keep the plants healthy, vigorous and shapely. Pruning is most important in the early years of a plant's life and many mature trees and shrubs need little pruning.

The basic equipment for pruning consists of a good pair of secateurs and a sharp knife. A sharp saw will be needed for tree pruning and a sealing compound such as Stockholm tar or Arbrex should be painted over the wounds left by any large cuts.

Try wherever possible to cut each branch away cleanly so that no stumps or ragged tears are left to harbour pests and diseases. If the complete removal of a branch is not practicable or desirable, always cut to an outward-facing bud. The cut should slope upwards to leave the bud at the apex. In all cases dead, diseased or crossing wood is cut out.

Evergreen shrubs do not need much pruning, any that does need doing being carried out in the early spring or if the shrubs are flowering then after they have finished flowering. I shorten the growths to ensure shapeliness where this is necessary. Conifers should not require any pruning usually. The freer growing forms such as this prostrate juniper may become invasive and these can be cut back with a pair of secateurs making clean cuts on the wood [1].

Deciduous shrubs can be divided into two groups. Those that flower in the spring or early summer produce their blooms on growths formed in the previous year. These are pruned immediately after flowering has finished to give them a chance to make new growths during the summer and autumn. These new shoots will then produce flowers the following year. The stems that have flowered are cut back to young shoots lower down the stems [2].

The second group comprises shrubs which flower during the summer and autumn on the current season's wood. These kinds are pruned in March or April to encourage plenty of young shoots to form so ensuring an abundance of flowers later in the year. Remove some of the oldest stems, particularly those that are not carrying much new growth and shorten the younger and stronger branches a little. With *Buddleia davidii* [3] and *Hydrangea paniculata*, I shorten all the branches down to within a few inches of ground level to encourage a few very strong new growths which will produce flower trusses of extra size.

Certain shrubs, especially some of the evergreens, require no more in the way of pruning than the removal of dead flower heads. It is best to remove the finished blooms before the seed pods are properly formed as seed production wastes the plant's energies and this will mean fewer flowers in the following year. Exceptions to this rule are those shrubs which have a crop of berries to follow the flowers and those from which you wish to propagate from seed. With rhododendrons and azaleas I twist off the clusters of seed pods [4], taking care not to damage the buds which are developing just below. I remove the old flower heads of lilacs with a pair of secateurs or a sharp knife [5], cutting them off at their bases. Heathers and lavenders can be lightly trimmed with a pair of shears after they have flowered but do not cut into the main shoots or old wood [6].

Shrubs and trees which have been grafted or budded on to a rootstock may throw up suckers from the stock. These

should be cut out with a sharp knife or a pair of secateurs at the point from which they arise [7,8,9]. The leaves of suckers are usually slightly different from those on the main growth and so they can be easily identified.

Trees do not need any regular pruning as most of them should be allowed to grow to their natural shapes. The only pruning I do is to remove any dead or diseased wood during the winter and possibly a badly placed or crossing branch [10]. If a large branch has to be removed this should be done in easy stages. First cut the branch from underneath for about a quarter of the way through the branch and then from above. This can be done about a foot away from the point of juncture with the main branch. It is then much easier to make a clean cut close to the main branch which can be pared smooth with a sharp knife [11]. The wound should be painted over with a bituminous tree paint to prevent the entry of diseases [12]. The pruning of ornamental cherries, peaches and plums is best carried out in the growing season after flowering, in June, July or August. At this time of the year the cuts heal quickly and there is less likelihood of them being infected by silver leaf disease.

Propagation The most common way of propagating trees and shrubs is by cuttings which can be of two types – half-ripe and hardwood. Shrubs which can be propagated by half-ripe cuttings include buddleia, caryopteris, ceanothus, cotoneaster, deutzia, escallonia, fuchsia, hebe, heathers, hydrangea, potentilla, rosemary, santolina, senecio, viburnum and weigela. The cuttings are taken during July, August and September from the current year's shoots. A shoot is ripe enough to take a cutting from when the lower portion can be bent without breaking.

The cuttings when prepared should be 6 to 8 in. long and I find it best to pull off the shoots with a heel of the older wood attached [1] and then trim this [2]. Heather cuttings are an exception being only 1 to 2 in. long. If the tip of a shoot is very soft then I cut it off. The leaves on the lower half of the cutting should be cut off with a sharp knife, close to the stem. For a rooting medium I prefer a mixture of equal parts by bulk of soil, peat and sand but for lime-hating shrubs such as the heathers a mixture of equal parts peat and sand is good.

Cuttings may be inserted in a cold frame, 2 in. apart, with half their length below the soil [3]. Dipping the base of

each cutting first into water and then in a hormone-rooting powder before insertion will assist root formation. A dibber can be used to make the planting holes and the cuttings must be firmly placed in the compost with their bases, especially, in close contact with the soil. After watering, the frame should be closed for three to four weeks only being opened once a day to remove any condensation. The cuttings should be syringed daily for the first two weeks to prevent them flagging. After about four weeks gradually increase the ventilation.

The young plants should be planted out in the nursery bed the following spring in rows 18 in. apart with the plants 12 in. apart in the rows. The following autumn many will be ready for planting into their permanent positions.

Half-ripe cuttings may also be rooted in pots – several being placed round the edge of each pot [4]. A polythene bag can then be inverted and secured over the top of the pot [5] but a heated propagating frame in a greenhouse is the ideal (page 127). They can also be rooted in a mist propagating unit. Cuttings rooted in this way must be gradually hardened off before they can be planted outside.

Hardwood cuttings are taken in the autumn from the current year's wood

which is well ripened and hard. *Cornus alba, C. stolonifera*, forsythia, garrya, laburnum, philadelphus, privet, ribes, sambucus, tamarix and willows are among the subjects which can be propagated in this way. I remove the shoots with a heel of older wood attached [6], trim this smooth and cut off the tip of the shoot just above a bud to give me a cutting 9 to 10 in. in length. Hardwood cuttings are rooted in the open ground in a sheltered corner. They should be inserted upright, 2 in. apart, in a trench to two-thirds of their length [7]. Place a layer of coarse sand along the bottom of the trench. The base of each cutting can be dipped in a hormone-rooting powder before insertion. Leave them in the rooting bed until the following autumn when they can be lifted and planted out into a nursery bed, about 1 ft. apart, in rows 2 ft. apart.

The hybrid trees and shrubs will not come true from seed but there is always a chance that an exciting new plant may be produced. Most seeds will be ripe and ready for harvesting during late summer and autumn. Store in a dry, frostproof place for the winter and sow in the spring. Fleshy berries and fruits, however, must be stratified during the winter preceding sowing in order to

soften the hard coats of the seeds. For this I take an old cocoa or coffee tin and make holes in the lid. I then place alternate layers of equal parts moist peat and sand and berries in the tin. Finally the tin is buried in the ground for the winter.

Another method of stratifying seeds is to put the berries between layers of moist peat and sand in clay pots and stand these against a north wall for the winter, protecting them from mice and other vermin with wire netting [8]. Only stratify one variety or species of seed in each tin or pot and label each carefully.

March is the best time to sow the seeds. Those stratified should be sifted from the peat and sand mixture and separated from the remains of their fleshy coverings. Then, together with the seeds which were stored dry, they can be sown either in seed boxes or in pots filled with John Innes seed compost. The containers are then placed in a cold frame or unheated greenhouse and should be kept well watered. Alternatively, some seeds may be sown in drills in a prepared bed in the open garden.

Layering means rooting shoots or branches while they are still attached to the parent plant and shrubs and trees

commonly propagated in this way include rhododendrons, viburnums, magnolias, kalmias, camellias, daphnes, lilacs and cotoneasters. I find the best time for doing this is in the spring but it can also be done during the summer too. Choose a branch or shoot of the previous year's growth that is near to the soil or which can easily be pulled down to soil level. Prepare the soil by forking it over and incorporating liberal quantities of peat and sand. Prepare the shoot by cutting a 2-in. long slit with a sharp knife, lengthways, halfway through it preferably at a joint [9]. This cut should be made 9 to 12in. from the tip of the shoot and can be dusted with a hormone rooting powder. It should be kept open with a spent match. Make a depression in the prepared soil about 3 to 4in. deep. The cut stem is pegged down into this hollow with a wire or wooden peg and covered with soil [10]. Tie the end of the shoot to a cane so that it is held in an upright position [11]. A large stone can be placed over the layered part of the branch to keep it firm and moist. Sever the layer after it has made a good root system. This may take one or two seasons.

Azaleas, rhododendrons, acers and magnolias can be air-layered in May and

early June. Select a shoot from the previous year's growth and make an incision as for normal layering. The cut is then dusted with a special hormone rooting powder and wrapped in wet sphagnum moss. Some moss should be pushed inside the cut to keep it open. The whole is covered with a polythene sleeve and this is sealed [12]. When the layer has rooted, white roots will be seen through the moss and it can then be severed from the parent plant and potted.

Shrubs can also be propagated by division in much the same way as described for herbaceous perennials. Shrubs and trees can also be propagated by budding and grafting but these techniques are too specialized to describe in this book.

ROSES

Container-grown plants can be transplanted at any time of the year, even in mid-summer, provided the soil is kept moist around the roots. This is because they will suffer very little root disturbance as do plants raised in the open ground.

Here I am planting a container-grown rose in a border which has been prepared in the same way as described on page 42. [1,2,3]. Before removing plants from containers they should be given a good watering. Tin containers will usually be split by the nurseryman with a special tool at the time of purchase but container-grown plants are also raised in pots of clay, plastic, treated paper or strong black polythene. Plants must be removed very carefully from their containers to prevent root damage.

Open-raised roses should be treated in the same way as deciduous shrubs and the planting technique is the same as described for the magnolia on page 26. The planting distances are usually recommended by the grower.

Roses are usually grafted or budded on to rootstocks. This process enables the grower to unite a garden rose with a root system or stock obtained from a wild or vigorous rose. The strength of the stock helps the more weakly and highly bred garden hybrids. When planting the union between the stock and the scion must be kept above soil level otherwise the scion will root and the beneficial properties of the rootstock will be lost. Roses can also be propagated by cuttings, layering and seed. See pages 34 and 35.

Standard and half-standard roses should be staked as described on page 26. All roses should be labelled with the name of their variety and each label should be tied firmly but loosely to the rose with a soft material [4]. These ties should be checked occasionally to ensure that they are not cutting into the roses.

When pruning, a good general rule to remember is that the more severely a branch is cut back the more vigorous will be the new shoots starting from it. The first pruning in the spring after planting is a simple one. I cut each sturdy growth of a bush rose to within about three buds of its base but I aim to make each cut just above an outward-pointing bud so that an open-centred bush will be formed [5]. Standard roses are treated just as though they were bushes perched on top of a tall stick. You may also need to remove any suckers which grow from the standard stem.

After the first year, pruning is as follows. The strong main growths of most hybrid tea roses should be shortened to within four, five or six buds of their bases and each sturdy side growth to one or two buds. Very old, weak, diseased or badly placed stems should be cut right out. Very vigorous roses must be treated more lightly. After removing old, worn-out and diseased wood, the strongest young growths should be left about 3 ft. in length, more weakly shoots being cut back a little further and laterals shortened to a few inches. Where bush roses are going to be cut back hard in March I have found no harm in cutting them back by about half in November. Although this means going over the bushes twice, I think that it prevents a lot of wind damage and root disturbance, especially in exposed areas.

Floribundas like a fairly light pruning. After cutting out all old, weak, diseased or dead wood the best of the younger stems are shortened by about a half [6], a few being cut back rather more severely, especially if the plant is not growing very strongly. The object is to make a fairly big, well-balanced bush with plenty of strong young growth to bear an abundance of flowers.

The shrub, species and old-fashioned

roses require very little systematic pruning except a thinning of the older wood in March. The pruning of climbing roses is described in the climbing plant section on page 40.

I often find it necessary to supplement pruning with a judicious thinning of the new shoots towards the end of April. Surplus shoots particularly those which look likely to grow inwards may be pinched out with the finger and thumb.

After pruning the rose bushes can be mulched with organic matter. Since roses are strong-growing plants they make a heavy demand on the food reserves in the soil and they should be regularly fed. A dressing of a slow-acting fertilizer such as bonemeal or hoof and horn at 4 to 6 oz. per sq. yd. should be applied in February [7] or September and forked lightly in [8]. A general quick-acting fertilizer or one that is specially prepared for roses should be given in March and further dressings applied at regular intervals throughout the spring and summer.

Be careful about watering during dry spells because once you start you must give enough water to penetrate right down into the soil and this must be repeated at regular intervals until there is a good rainfall.

Faded flowers should be removed to encourage the production of further flowers. If all the flowers on a stem fade together, the stem can be cut back 8 or 9 in. to encourage the growth of strong new shoots and a second crop of bloom [9].

Suckers may grow from the roots below the union of the rose and the rootstock and should be removed at the point of origin [10]. They can usually be easily recognized. In the autumn gather the debris from the soil around the roses and burn it. Weeds can be controlled by chemical means [11].

Roses suffer from a number of pests and diseases and a careful watch must be kept for them so that if they do appear action may be taken to control them [12]. Greenfly can be troublesome from early May onwards and if they are seen the bushes should be sprayed immediately with BHC, derris, malathion or menazon. A winter spray of 3 per cent. tar oil should be applied to those bushes which were badly infected the previous summer. Caterpillars can be controlled by BHC, derris or trichlorphon. Hand picking can also be carried out.

Occasionally spraying with BHC will control leafhoppers. These suck the sap from the leaves and cause them to become pale and mottled. Leafhoppers

shed their skins and the white moulted skins will be visible on the under surfaces of the leaves. Some sawflies reduce the leaves to a skeleton while others cause them to roll up tightly. Spraying with BHC will help but the leaf-rolling sawflies are well protected inside the leaves and may escape. Thrips are responsible for the buds turning brown. Infected buds should be removed and the plants sprayed with BHC.

The best way of keeping roses free from diseases is by good cultivation and by allowing plenty of free air to circulate round the bushes. The three most common diseases need no descriptions. These are mildew, black spot and rust. Mildew is best controlled by making preventive sprays throughout June, July and August with dinocap and Bordeaux mixture. For black spot spray at least once a fortnight with captan throughout late spring and summer. Rust is controlled by preventive spraying with Bordeaux mixture, thiram and zineb.

Die-back is caused by grey mould fungus. Dark brownish-purple patches appear on the branches and the whole stem above these dies. All dead and discoloured growth should be cut out and the plants sprayed with Bordeaux mixture.

Climbing and Hedging Plants

No well-planned garden should be without a selection of climbing plants and under this heading I have included those slightly tender shrubs which may be damaged by frost when grown in the open border but which will thrive when given the added protection of a wall. Climbing roses, too, are dealt with in this section.

When choosing climbing plants for walls the aspect must be considered. Plants grown against north-facing walls will get little direct sunshine whereas those grown on south-facing walls may get an excess of warmth and those on east-facing walls may be exposed to cold winds. However, there are very many climbing and wall plants to choose from and some can be found to suit every situation. Try and match the colour of brick walls with the colours of the plants to be grown. The neutral colour of most stone means that it mixes well with almost anything but red bricks may be difficult.

Climbers need not be confined to house walls. They can be grown up garages and sheds, over fences, pergolas, arches and other structures and will disguise old tree stumps. Several climbers and wall plants may be grown close together to produce a longer show of colour and lovely effects are achieved when two climbers, which flower at the same time, are grown so that their stems entwine.

Most gardeners prefer a screen of some kind around their garden and a hedge will make a far more pleasing and natural background to the flowers and other plants than a fence. Hedges may also be planted within the garden to screen off the kitchen garden or compost heap and some hedging plants make excellent windbreaks for sheltering other plantings and the house from prevailing winds. Evergreen shrubs will make better boundary hedges than those which are deciduous but whichever shrub you choose it should have some distinguishing feature such as handsome leaves, flowers or berries. A hedging shrub should be well suited to the soil and climatic conditions for a mistake in this respect can be costly and an unhealthy hedge can ruin the appearance of the whole garden. It should also be thick enough to give shelter without constant attention.

CLIMBERS

Planting The planting beds for climbers and wall shrubs should be at least 18 in. wide. Where concrete or paving goes up to the house walls climbers can be planted in tubs or other suitable containers provided they are well cared for in respect to feeding and watering but their growth will be less prolific. The soil around the walls of a house is often poor and should be well worked and prepared down to a depth of 15 in. Sometimes it needs to be replaced completely with soil from a more fertile part of the garden.

A very important point to watch out for when planting climbers and wall shrubs against a house wall is to be certain that they will receive enough water. Often there is an overhang on the roof which prevents them from getting their fair share of rainwater. Plant with the roots of the climber well spread out away from the wall and make regular inspections with a watering-can to see that none of your plants are suffering from drought. Be careful, too, not to plant where drips are likely to occur from overflow pipes.

Here I am preparing the border round a pergola and planting a container-grown honeysuckle to train up the structure. There is greater freedom of space when planting against a structure such as this rather than against a wall. The soil is usually of a better quality and there are not the same dangers with regard to overhangs and overflow pipes. The turf is lifted [1] and the soil dug over [2] and organic matter incorporated [3]. The honeysuckle is carefully removed from its container [4] and positioned in its hole [5]. It is firmly planted. Note the distance which I am planting from the pergola post [6]. Other climbers which I grow over the pergola are the lovely white rose Madame Alfred Carrière, the carmine-pink thornless rose Zéphirine Drouhin, wisteria and clematis to provide a continuous show over a long period. I also grow the passion flower in a sheltered corner [7]. Here I am tying in the new shoots of one of my climbing roses loosely with raffia [8].

Training Some climbers are self-supporting and will cling to walls naturally like the ivy with its aerial roots and the virginia creeper with its tiny sucker pads. Others climb by tendrils, twining stems and leaf stalks when they are provided with some sort of support. Wall shrubs, which are not true climbers, will need to be tied to their supports. Plastic-covered wire netting [9] can be bought from many garden sundriesmen.

A wooden trellis can be made and mounted about 3 in. away from the wall to allow for a free circulation of air behind the plants. This is especially important where climbing plants such as roses, which are very susceptible to mildew, are to be grown. Lengths of medium-gauge galvanized wire can be stretched either horizontally or vertically at 1-ft. intervals and attached to the wall surface by vine eyes or wire strainers [10,11].

All ties should be made loosely to allow the stems and branches to expand in girth and should be made with a soft material like soft string or raffia to prevent chafing. Ties should be inspected during pruning to make sure that the plants are not being strangled.

Wall shrubs like pyracantha and *Cotoneaster horizontalis* are not self-clinging but provided they are given a minimum of support and judicious pruning they will mould themselves to the surface of the wall on which they are grown [12]. Shorten all the side growths to 6 to 8 in. directly they begin to get really hard and woody at the base which is usually between June and August but take care not to remove the young berries of any of the berrying shrubs while doing this. This specimen of *Cotoneaster conspicua* [13] has been planted to give root shade to the clematis for although clematis like to have their flowers in the sun they also like a cool root run.

Aftercare Otherwise the aftercare and propagation of climbers and wall shrubs follows the same lines as that for a shrub in the open border in respect to mulching, feeding [14] and weed control but a special watch will have to be kept for pests and especially diseases which may spread rapidly in the more confined spaces. Wall shrubs, such as this *Camellia williamsii*, should be dead-headed [15].

Pruning For the purposes of pruning climbers fall into much the same groups as shrubs although true climbers tend to be spoiled by much pruning. The early flowerers are trimmed and shortened after the last of their blooms have faded and those that flower during the summer are pruned in February [16].

I prune my climbing roses in February cutting out some of the old wood and leaving as much young wood as possible.

HEDGES

Planting The planting times for hedges are the same as those detailed for shrubs on page 26 and the preparation of the soil is similar to that necessary for a shrub or rose border. A border at least one yard wide should be dug as far in advance of the planting date as possible. This gives the soil time to settle well and allows any organic matter which may have been incorporated time to start breaking down and releasing plant foods. It is usually sufficient to single dig to the depth of a spade the length of the area to receive the hedge but if the soil is inclined to be wet and hold water deeper cultivation is advisable. Well-rotted farmyard manure, garden compost, moist peat, leafmould, spent hops, shoddy and other similar organic material should be incorporated in the bottom of the trench as the digging proceeds. After digging I like to fork a slow-acting fertilizer into the top few inches of the soil at the rate of 2 to 4oz. per sq. yd. This releases plant foods over a long period, thereby supplying the hedge with the necessary nutrients. If hedging plants arrive when you are unable to plant because of bad weather or lack of time treat as advised on page 82.

There are two methods of planting a hedge. Either take out a trench 15 to 18in. wide to run the length of the intended hedge or dig individual planting holes. The choice rather depends on the recommended planting distance. If the individuals in the hedge need to be planted 18in. apart or closer, then a trench is perhaps the easiest way. For larger specimens, which will be planted 2ft. or more apart, individual planting holes are less time consuming and involve less work. Here are some recommended planting distances – privet and quickthorn, 9 to 12in. apart; *Lonicera nitida*, beech and hornbeam, 12 to 15in. apart; yew and holly, 18 to 24in. apart; cupressocyparis and thuya, 2 to 3ft. apart.

Here I am planting a *Cupressocyparis leylandii* hedge within my garden as a windbreak and I am digging individual planting holes [1,2,3,4]. The canes mark the position of each plant. Whichever way you choose to plant your hedge do make sure that the roots of each shrub are well spread out and that they are planted to the same depth that they were in the nursery or container. The uppermost roots should be covered with 2 to 3in. of soil. Plant firmly and either stake each individual shrub or tie them

loosely to horizontally trained wires to prevent windrock until they are established.

An annual mulch should be given every spring of organic matter and an annual feed with a good balanced fertilizer should also be applied.

Trimming Formal hedges should be kept regularly trimmed so that they remain shapely and well covered with foliage. Do not allow a formal hedge to get out of hand before trimming as the hard cutting back which will then be needed will sometimes ruin the appearance of the hedge. Informal hedges do not need regular treatment but I go over them occasionally with a pair of secateurs to remove any long or straggly growths. Flowering hedges should not be trimmed too hard or they will produce few flowers. A pair of garden shears [5] or an electric trimmer [6] are the most suitable tools for trimming the majority of formal hedges. However, for large-leaved evergreen types, such as aucuba, rhododendrons and laurels, trimming is best carried out with secateurs so that the cuts are made on the wood. If such hedging plants are trimmed with shears the leaves will be cut and will turn brown at the edges.

Hedging plants There is a wide choice of hedging and screening plants to suit all soils and sites. If you want a long stretch of hedge requiring a large number of plants then you might like to choose from quickthorn, privet, beech, hornbeam and lonicera which are, on the whole, the least expensive. In my own garden I have beech hedges on the road side and within the garden to provide a backdrop to a border at the side of the drive and to screen off the vegetable garden. Beech is really as effective as an evergreen for hedging purposes for the green leaves turn brown in late autumn and are retained throughout the winter bringing colour and warmth to the garden.

For a fast-growing hedge nothing can beat *Cupressocyparis leylandii* which will produce a deep green hedge up to 25 ft. tall in a few years. Other attractive conifers include *Chamaecyparis lawsoniae*, Lawson's cypress and its many varieties including Green Hedger, and *Thuya plicata*. Evergreen shrubs which make good hedging plants include many members of the berberis [1] and cotoneaster families. Holly, although slow growing, makes a handsome hedge [2] especially when the variegated species are planted as does the quicker-growing laurel (*Prunus laurocerasus*) [3].

Of the flowering hedges rhododendrons are a good choice for an acid soil for apart from their beautiful flowers they provide a barrier of handsome, evergreen foliage. Roses are very popular hedging subjects [4] and good varieties include *Rosa rugosa* which will make a really big hedge and provide a display of flowers for many weeks in summer; the hybrid tea rose Peace with pale to deep yellow flowers marked with cerise-pink on the edges of the petals and the floribundas Queen Elizabeth, soft pink; Iceberg, white; Chinatown, yellow; and Shepherd's Delight, red, orange and yellow. There are also good shrub roses for hedging too. Fuchsias and escallonias [5] grow well in the milder seaside areas.

Splendid shrubs for low hedges within the garden include *Lonicera nitida*, *Buxus sempervirens*, *Berberis thunbergii*, rosemary, lavender [6] and some heathers.

Flower Gardening

Here I am concerned with the cultivation of herbaceous perennials, annuals, biennials, bulbs and bedding plants which provide us with such a lovely succession of flowers. I have grouped them together in this one chapter partly for reasons of space and partly because these plants are often grown together in mixed borders and beds along with trees and shrubs to give, with skilful planting, year-round interest and colour.

I often think that there is more scope for the exercise of ingenuity in the design of flower borders and beds than any other feature in the garden for their shapes and sizes can be infinitely varied to suit the circumstances and as far as planting goes there are many thousands of plants from which to choose. I consider that it is a mistake to give a border or bed a straight edge for this is harsh and out of place in the informal setting which these features demand. Much more pleasing is to curve the edge so that the plants are brought right out into the grass.

When working out planting schemes it is more important to place plants so that they form pleasing shapes and patterns than it is to get perfect colour blendings. You will notice that the colours of flowers seldom clash as do manufactured colourings and it is largely a matter of taste and experience which colours you plant alongside each other. I always try to arrange things so that early-flowering plants which may be dull or even unsightly for the rest of the season are reasonably well masked by later-flowering plants.

Always make bold plantings of each individual species or variety so that each stands out well against the other and vary the shape of each group to prevent uniformity. Vary the heights of each group, too, within reason. For a border which is viewed from the front only, plant the taller subjects at the back and the smaller ones along the front edge. The plants in a bed which is viewed from all sides should be of a more equal height with the taller plants in the middle.

HERBACEOUS PERENNIALS

Planting March and April are the most favourable months of the year to plant herbaceous perennials although when weather conditions are good I like to start this job in February. They can also be planted towards the end of September and during the first half of October but this might not be quite so successful especially on heavy soils which can become very wet and cold in the autumn. However, peonies, kniphofias, hellebores and other plants which are slow to become established may benefit from being planted at this time of the year since they may be badly affected by dry spells after a spring planting.

I like to prepare the planting holes for the smaller plants with a trowel [1] but for the rest, of course, I use a spade [2]. The planting hole should be wide and deep enough to take the roots of the plant when they are well spread out. It is important to work the soil firmly around the roots for if they do not come into close contact with the soil, they will wither and die [3]. The depth of planting is also critical. Cover the old soil mark by about $\frac{1}{2}$ in. and make sure that the top roots are covered by 1 in. of soil. The crown of the plant – the place from which most of the basal shoots grow –

should be at or just below soil level. The spacing will vary according to the habit of the plant but a good general rule is to space edging plants 6 to 9 in. apart, those for the middle of the border 12 to 18 in. apart and those for the back 2 to 3 ft. apart.

Herbaceous perennials should never be planted when the soil is wet and cold but it may be necessary to plant when the weather and soil are dry. If this is the case water them well after planting with a watering-can. The spout of the can should have sacking wrapped around the top of it to break the rush of water. When a rose is used to deliver the water gently, the surface of the soil soon becomes deceptively wet but the water may not penetrate through and the lower areas will still be very dry.

Staking, thinning, weeding, forking over the soil, removing dead flowers to encourage further flowering, feeding with slow-acting fertilizers, and, of course, lifting and dividing every three or four years – these are the jobs which we must attend to whenever we grow perennial flowers.

Staking My favourite way of staking herbaceous plants is by using last year's peasticks from the vegetable garden [4]. For a plant say $2\frac{1}{2}$ ft. tall I put peasticks,

which are $1\frac{1}{2}$ to 2 ft. tall, all around the clump and if these make the border look like a timber yard when they are first put in I know that by the middle of June they will be completely hidden from view. The plants grow up through the sticks and are given all the support they could possibly want. Peasticks are, however, becoming increasingly difficult to buy but twiggy branches are a good substitute. I press these firmly into the ground and then trim them to the required height [5].

Delphiniums and lupins I stake individually with bamboo canes using a soft material such as raffia, fillis or twine to secure each spike to the cane. So that each stem can expand and also move slightly with the wind I take the tying material round the stake, knot it and then take it loosely round the stem, knotting it again. (Page 55.)

Aftercare The most important time to work over the soil in between the plants, without of course disturbing the plant roots, is just before growth gets into its stride in spring [6], and this is the time, too, to work in a light dressing of a slow-acting fertilizer like bonemeal or hoof and horn [7]. Never feed flowering plants with quick-acting fertilizers or unwanted growth will be produced at the

expense of the flowers. A mulch of peat can be given after the feed [8]. This mulch will conserve moisture and suppress weeds.

Dead-heading is removing the flowers as soon as they have faded [9]. This often encourages plants to produce another crop of flowers and, of course, it keeps the border tidy.

If tall bearded iris are grown, cut down the foliage to within about 6 in. of the ground in the autumn to lessen the chances of damage from disease, and with delphiniums cut back the stems almost to ground level at the end of the season and cover the crowns of the plants with well-weathered ashes [10] as a protection against winter damp. The crowns of the kniphofias get useful protection from tying the leaves together at this same time. The border will look neater and will be healthier if all the persistent dead and straggly growth is cut down in winter [11].

If you are a newcomer to gardening, thinning [12] is a task which you will do with some misgivings but you will soon discover how rewarding it is. For example, if you reduce the growths on each delphinium plant to about six, it will be found that the spikes are far superior to those on plants left unthinned.

Perennial flowers are largely untouched by pests and diseases and provided the growing conditions are good and any dead plant material and debris is cleared away you should have little trouble.

Three to four years after planting, perennials start to look straggly and weak and the quality of the flowers will fall off. This is due to the exhaustion of the plants and the gradual depletion of food reserves in the soil. It is then that the plants need lifting and dividing. After the plants have been lifted, either in the spring or autumn, the soil in the border can be improved by the addition of compost or other humus-forming material. I also apply a dressing of bonemeal, followed by one of a good all-purpose fertilizer before replanting. It is then that you can give the border a completely fresh appearance by having a general reshuffle and creating new plant associations. This can give the garden a distinctive new look.

Propagation The most usual way of increasing herbaceous perennial plants is by division of the roots in spring or autumn. Most herbaceous plants can be divided simply by pulling them apart with the hands. Each division should have healthy roots and at least three or four shoots. The retained portions always come from the outside of the clump, the woody and older centres being discarded altogether. Here I am dividing a clump of herbaceous iris [1,2].

Some plants demand tougher treatment. These should be lifted with a spade and then two forks, placed back to back, are pushed into the centre of each clump. The fork handles are then pressed outwards which will loosen the roots [3,4]. Any reluctant parts can be cut with a sharp knife.

The divisions to be replanted should be out of the ground as short a time as possible and they should be covered with sacking or some other material to avoid drying out by sun or wind.

Propagation by root cuttings is the best way of increasing many thick-rooted perennials like verbascums, oriental poppies, phlox, anchusa and statice. Some fibrous-rooted plants, like the gaillardias, may also be readily increased in this way. Root cuttings are best taken during the first six months of the year. The plants from which the cuttings are required are lifted and the roots are washed. The length of each cutting varies from 1 to 3 in. depending on the thickness of the roots, the shorter cuttings being the thickest. They can be inserted in boxes or pots of free-draining compost – John Innes seed compost (page 122) or an equal mixture of peat and sand will do very well – in either of two ways. Thick cuttings like those of anchusa should be cut so that the base end is slanting so that it is easily distinguished. These are then inserted into the compost so that the tops are just covered [5]. Thin cuttings can be laid on the surface of the compost and covered with a thin layer of the same mixture [6]. The cuttings are then watered in and placed in a garden frame or a sheltered part of the garden. Once the cuttings have made growth they are potted on, or reboxed and grown on for subsequent planting out.

Herbaceous perennials can also be increased by seed and softwood cuttings.

Very many lovely combinations of plants are possible in the flower border. Here are lupins and the herbaceous geranium

ANNUALS AND BIENNIALS

Hardy annuals The term hardy annual is used to describe any annual flower which can be raised from seed sown in the open ground in spring and which needs no protection whatever during its cycle of growth. Quite a few can even be sown in the open ground in August or September to come into flower in late spring and early summer. Calendulas, larkspurs, nigella, godetias and sweet peas are some of the annuals often grown in this way.

Annuals prefer a well-drained, light soil and plenty of sunshine but will grow in most soils provided they are not heavy, wet and cold when germination will be poor, or very rich when too much leafy growth will be produced at the expense of the flowers. The only fertilizer I would give would be a light dressing of bonemeal some weeks before sowing.

The key to success with annuals is the preparation of the seed bed which must be weed free and worked to a fine tilth. Sowing can be done during the latter half of March in warmer districts but gardeners in colder areas would be advised to wait until late April or early May. Always choose a fine still day for sowing.

With small seeds I like to sow with my finger and thumb, holding the seeds in the palm of my left hand and just lightly sprinkling them over the ground with my right. I find that this allows me to sow thinly and reasonably accurately. Afterwards I rake the seeds into the surface soil. Sowing broadcast, though, has its disadvantages for weeding can be very difficult. A better way if the ground is known to be weedy is to sow in prepared drills which can be weeded and thinned much more easily [1]. If this method is used the depth of the drills will have to be adjusted to the size of the seed being sown, the smallest only having just a light covering of soil and the largest as much as $1\frac{1}{2}$ to 2 in.

Make the first thinning as soon as the seedlings can be conveniently handled, then two to three weeks later make the final thinning to leave the smallest-growing annuals 9 in. apart and the taller varieties 15 to 18 in. apart [2]. In showery weather during May and early June it is quite possible to lift some of the plants, if this is done carefully, and replant them successfully where there are gaps.

Weeding can be done either by hand or gently with a hoe [3]. It is important not to disturb the developing roots of the annuals. During dry weather it will be necessary to water. Taller annuals will need staking and I use twiggy pieces of birch [4]. Dead-head the plants regularly while they are flowering to encourage the production of further flowers [5].

Biennials The seed of biennials, and those plants treated as biennials, should be sown out of doors in the second half of May or in early June in a prepared seed bed, the surface of which has been raked down to a fine tilth before sowing. As soon as they have made their first or second pair of true leaves, the seedlings are transferred to a nursery bed or, where there is insufficient space for this, to an odd corner of the garden where they can be grown on until they are ready for planting out in their flowering positions [6]. Spring and early summer flowering biennials are planted the previous autumn, summer-flowerers are planted in the autumn or spring.

Half-hardy annuals Half-hardy annuals cannot be planted out in the open garden until all danger of frost has passed. They can be raised by the gardener in one of three ways. They can be sown in boxes in a greenhouse heated to 13°C. (55°F.) or they can be sown in the open ground in spring and covered with cloches until the end of May, or some can be sown where they are to flower in early May so that they will not have germinated until the weather is safe. Boxes of half-hardy annuals are also sold by garden sundriesmen and some greengrocers but in my opinion these come on to the market too early in the year for these tender annuals should not be planted out until the end of May or early June.

Sowing in a greenhouse or heated frame should begin in late February with antirrhinums, lobelias, salvias, ageratums, *Begonia semperflorens*, nicotianas, petunias and verbenas. Late March is early enough for stocks, asters, French and African marigolds, nemesias, alyssum and cosmeas for these germinate and grow rapidly.

Clean seed boxes should be used and for better drainage place some pieces of broken clay pot, if these are available, in the bottom and then cover these with a layer of peat [1]. This will prevent the water draining through too rapidly before it has time to soak in and will also help to keep the soil sweet. Add the compost [2] – I consider John Innes seed compost (page 122) still the best for this – and firm it down well with the fingers [3]. Fill the box to within one inch of the top and press down for a flat level surface with a wooden press [4] or the bottom of another box. Water gently but thoroughly with a rose fitted to a watering-can. Then sow the seeds thinly [5] and cover with a sprinkling of soil. Cover the box with a sheet of glass and some paper [6] – newspaper will do very well – and leave on a greenhouse shelf until the seeds have germinated. Remove the glass and paper and grow on until the seedlings are ready to be pricked out. Be careful at this stage not to let the seedlings become scorched from the sun.

Prick out into boxes or pots of John Innes potting compost No. 1 or one of the loamless composts so that the seedlings are spaced 2 in. apart each way [7]. Grow on until they are well established and then gradually harden off (page 120) before planting out in late May or early June. Toss the young plants out of their boxes and separate off each plant [8].

BEDDING OUT

Bedding out means planting for a short term or seasonal display. In public parks and large gardens bedding plants are renewed several times during the year to provide a continuous show of colour but owners of smaller gardens need only concern themselves with spring and summer bedding. Spring bedding is usually planted out the previous autumn and consists of biennials such as wallflowers, double daisies and forget-me-nots and bulbs, chiefly tulips, daffodils and hyacinths. Summer bedding is planted out after the spring bedding is over in late May and June and the most popular schemes include half-hardy annuals, half-hardy perennials (raised in a similar way to half-hardy annuals and discarded at the end of the season) and some greenhouse plants such as fuchsias and geraniums (pelargoniums).

Cuttings of such plants as fuchsias and pelargoniums may be taken in August and September from the plants in the summer beds. Firm, non-flowering shoots are best and the cuttings should be 3 to 4 in. long. Each is cut straight through at the bottom, just below a joint where a leaf or leaves are attached to the stem. The bottom leaves are removed and the base of each cutting is dipped in

a hormone-rooting powder. The cuttings are inserted in holes about 1 in. deep made with a dibber in sandy soil. A good compost for cuttings consists of equal parts by volume of soil, coarse sand and peat but quite a lot will root in ordinary garden soil with a little sand and peat raked in. Every August I root some geranium cuttings out of doors without any protection at all but by September it is better to put the cuttings in pots [1,2,3] or boxes so that they can be brought into a frostproof greenhouse or frame directly frost threatens. Geranium and fuchsia cuttings root very quickly and indicate when they have done so by starting to grow again. This is the signal to tap them out of the pots and boxes or lift them from the border outside and pot them individually into small pots – 2½ in. for fuchsias, 3 to 3½ in. for geraniums. John Innes potting compost or one of the loamless composts should be used. Stand the pots on a shelf or staging in the greenhouse to grow on. Cuttings will also root readily in March and April.

The planting procedure for spring and summer bedding plants is much the same as for perennials (page 46) [4]. Where bulbs are to be used plant the bedding plants first and then the bulbs using a trowel [5].

I am especially fond of fuchsias and though I grow a great many as bushes I also grow a lot of standards. To do this take cuttings in August and when they have rooted and have been potted, place a cane to each plant and keep the main growth tied to this so that it is absolutely straight and erect [6]. All the side growths are removed until the main stem is 5 ft. high. The top of the plant is then tipped out to make it branch. About six to eight good branches are allowed to develop and when these are 6 to 8 in. long they are pinched again. Greenhouse cultivation is necessary for this and the temperature should be kept at 13°C. (55°F.). Plant out with the other summer bedding plants to give height and water well throughout the summer.

There are other plants, naturally low growing, which can be made even more useful by a little training and pegging down. This can be done with annual phlox, verbena and ivy-leaved geraniums. If some fairly stout galvanized wire is cut into 6-in. lengths and these are bent like hairpins, they can be put over the trailing shoots and pushed into the soil to hold them where they are required to cover the soil with a continuous carpet of growth and flowers.

No flowers are so welcome in the spring as the daffodils and they hold a special place in our affections

BULBS

There is not the space here to go into the botanical differences between bulbs, corms and tubers which are all underground storage organs collectively known by gardeners as bulbs but it is not necessary to explain these differences in such a basic guide.

Naturalized bulbs are those grown under as near natural conditions as possible. They are eminently suitable for informal gardens where they can be grown under trees and down banks or in variety in a woodland area. How about planting daffodils under an apple tree, muscari round a flowering cherry so that the blue flowers of the muscari are at their best when the cherry is at full blossom or crocuses and anemones down banks? Not only do these plantings look lovely but they demand very little cultural attention once planted. In my own garden, in March, I find this planting of forsythia and daffodil Golden Harvest very welcoming [1].

There is one aspect of growing naturalized bulbs, however, which must be considered by the owners of small gardens. The grass must not be cut until the foliage of the bulbs has died down naturally. The reason for this is that the bulbs cannot flourish if they are not allowed to complete their growth and store up food resources for the next season's development. The grass when eventually cut may be an unattractive brown colour but watering and feeding with a lawn fertilizer will soon bring the colour back to normal.

Naturalized bulbs should be planted in drifts, not in rows or rigid clumps. The best way of achieving a good effect is to scatter handfuls of bulbs and plant them where they fall [2]. The easiest way of planting naturalized bulbs is with a special tool known as a bulb planter. This cuts out a core of turf and soil when it is pressed into the ground and removes it intact when it is given a twist and lift. The bulb is then placed in the hole [3] and the core of soil and turf replaced and firmed with the feet. Small quantities of bulbs can be planted with a trowel. Where only a small area is involved the turf can be lifted, the soil improved with a dressing of bonemeal at the rate of 2 oz. to the sq. yd., the bulbs planted and the turf replaced [4] but this can develop into a tedious, time-consuming task.

Bulbs can also be grown to great advantage in the mixed border and those that look especially well in such a setting include lilies, gladioli, the crown imperials, *Galtonia candicans*, tuberous ranunculus, montbretias, ixias, tigridias, camassias, and English and Spanish irises. Borders for bulbs should be well worked and because the drainage must be good a dressing of well-saturated horticultural peat should be forked in. A dressing of bonemeal or hoof and horn at the rate of 4 oz. to the sq. yd. can be given with the peat. Fresh manure should never be placed in direct contact with bulbs but it can be profitably incorporated below planting level. Bulbs are generally planted with a trowel [5].

Planting depths and distances vary considerably for different bulbs, corms and tubers and it is difficult in the space allowed here to give much guide. It is perhaps best to inquire when purchasing the bulbs about what depth and distance they need to be planted but when in doubt a good general rule is to ensure that the bulb is covered with twice its own depth of soil and is no nearer to its neighbour than the height of the mature flowering stem. Planting times, too, depend on the plant in question but it is better to plant too early than too late. Bulbs which are sensitive to moisture as for example gladioli and lilies should be bedded on sand when they are planted. Some of the taller bulbs

such as the lilies will need staking. Firmly secure one bamboo cane to each plant in the ground and tie the flower stem to this loosely with a soft material. The plant should be allowed some freedom of movement in the wind or it will look unnatural [6].

It is important that after a bulb has flowered its foliage is allowed to die down naturally. If the space is required in the bed for other subjects, especially where bulbs have been planted for spring bedding or if the bulbs are likely to be damaged by frost the following winter, then they should be carefully dug up and heeled in in another part of the garden until the foliage has died down [7]. The bulbs can then be stored in trays in an airy frostproof place until planting time comes round again [8]. Before storing the bulbs should be cleaned and any diseased specimens should be destroyed. It is better, however, for the majority of bulbs to be left in situ wherever possible for several years without disturbing them. A layer of peat or straw over the soil will afford some protection to the less hardy species and varieties [9]. Bulbs which have been grown as pot plants for the house may be planted outside when they have finished flowering. They should flower the following year out of doors [10].

When planting bulbs in carefully planned formal schemes, special attention has to be paid to the height, colour and flowering time of the chosen subjects for the appearance can be ruined if the bulbs flower at different times, are of uneven height and miscellaneous colours.

Early Single, Early Double, Cottage, Broken and Darwin tulips are especially well suited for bedding as are hyacinths. In addition there are some narcissi, galanthus, crocuses, muscari, chionodoxas and scillas which adapt to this formal treatment. Many bulbs make a very colourful display when planted in beds on their own but others such as the daffodils and tulips are often very effectively combined with other spring flowers. It is best to plant the bedding plants first and then put in the bulbs using a trowel.

Flower beds against walls with a warm south or west aspect are ideal for growing a selection of the less hardy, sun-loving bulbous subjects. These include the handsome pink *Nerine bowdenii* [11], the orange-red *Crocosmia masonorum*, modern hybrid montbretias, *Iphelon uniflorum*, *Acidanthera bicolor murieliae* [12] and *Amarylis belladonna*.

Bulbs in containers Growing bulbs in tubs and other containers has, apart from anything else, one unusual advantage for the plants can be moved at will from one position in the garden to another. They are excellent on a terrace or patio where they will add colour and interest especially in the early spring [1,2].

Bulbs are good window box plants and although I prefer to see these boxes devoted to one kind of flower rather than to a mixture, there is no reason why daffodils and muscari, or other similar combinations, should not look very well together. Daffodils, tulips, crocuses and hyacinths are all popular window box plants.

Tubs give more scope than window boxes because of their greater depth and tall daffodils and tulips look more in proportion in such containers. I have found tubs excellent for lilies notably the popular regal lily, *Lilium regale* and the Madonna lily, *L. candidum*.

A method of growing daffodils which I have found especially successful is that of planting a double layer of the bulbs in a deep tub. This gives a tremendous concentration of colour in a small area. I use John Innes potting compost No. 2 in tubs at least 12 in. deep. It is important to make sure that there are sufficient holes in the bases of the tubs to ensure good drainage. Place a layer of crocks over the drainage holes and cover these with roughage. Add a layer of compost and set the first layer of bulbs in position [3]. Cover the bulbs with compost so that the tips are just showing [4] and then position the second layer of bulbs between the tips of the first layer [5]. Work in compost among these bulbs and make this firm [6].

I, especially, like to see daffodils in a green tub with the supporting bands painted black and multi-coloured tulips in a white tub with black banding.

For house display it is usual to plant in ornamental bowls without drainage holes so that no water can trickle out and damage the furniture. Ordinary composts will quickly become sour in these bowls and so I would advise you to buy bulb fibre which should be thoroughly moistened before use. For greenhouse display the more conventional pots and compost can be used. Set the bulbs evenly and closely (but not touching) on a layer of compost and barely cover with more compost. Water well and then place the bowls in a cool, dark place or plunge outside by standing on gravel or concrete and covering three to four inches deep with peat. Leave for eight to ten weeks and then bring out into a light room or into the greenhouse. Stake if necessary and water.

More advice on growing plants in containers is given on page 59.

Patios are now a common feature of many homes and they will be enhanced by the inclusion
of tubs filled with gaily coloured bedding plants

Hanging baskets Hanging baskets, made from stout galvanized wire or plastic, can be bought from garden shops and hardware stores. They are bowl shaped, from 10 to 18 in. in diameter and are suspended by chains. They are usually made up in May or early June for summer display in a sheltered but sunny part of the garden or greenhouse and dismantled in October but a more permanent planting can be obtained with hardy creeping plants such as the large and small-leaved periwinkles (*Vinca major* and *V. minor*), creeping jenny (*Lysimachia nummularia*), ferns and variegated ivies.

For a temporary display during the summer months, however, any of the plants commonly used for summer bedding can be planted in a hanging basket including pelargoniums, fuchsias, dwarf nasturtiums, lobelias and petunias. *Campanula isophylla*, a slightly tender, trailing, perennial bellflower with blue or white flowers can also be very pretty and the various ornamental forms of asparagus, ivy, tradescantia and zebrina are striking. There are also pendulous varieties of begonia which are valuable.

The baskets are lined either with black polythene, which has holes slit for drainage, or moss which is more attractive [1]. This lining prevents the compost from being washed out. John Innes potting compost No. 3 can be used [2] or one of the soilless composts and the plants chosen to trail round the sides are planted on their sides [3,4]. An upright growing plant such as a zonal pelargonium or a fuchsia can be planted in the centre of each basket [5]. Do not overfill the basket while planting because the plants will grow during the summer and will soon fill the basket. After planting water well and hang up to drain. If you have a greenhouse put the basket in there for a week or ten days to settle and become established before hanging outside.

As many of the plants commonly used in hanging baskets are tender, it is usually unsafe to put such baskets out of doors before the end of May. During the summer, plants in hanging baskets must be watered regularly and freely. They should be given a liquid feed every week to 10 days. Dead-head the flowers [6] and keep a watch out for pests and diseases.

Ornamental containers Tubs, troughs and other ornamental containers can be used on paved areas and patios and filled with spring and then summer-flowering plants. They are made from stone, wood, pottery, concrete, metal or plastic. Lead was once largely used, beaten or cast in elaborate designs, but this has become too expensive for most people. However, excellent reproductions of old lead vases and troughs made from fibreglass or plastic can be bought and these are both light and durable. Barrels, sawn in half, make excellent tubs. The insides of wooden containers must be charred or treated with a harmless wood preservative. Creosote should not be used as this gives off toxic fumes.

Drainage is an important consideration when planting in these ornamental containers and there should be adequate holes to allow the surplus water to escape. These will either be at the bottom of the sides of the container when the container may stand on the ground or they will be in the bottom of the container itself. In this case the container must be raised a little from the ground to allow the water to escape easily.

A John Innes compost can be used or one of those based on peat and if possible the compost should be changed annually. If the compost is not changed annually it should be fed after the first year with a good all-round fertilizer before replanting.

Bedding plants again come into their own for planting in these ornamental containers. Here I am planting pelargoniums for a summer display using a trowel [1]. Some plants should be trailed over the side of the container to present a better balance [2]. Good permanent plants for containers include agapanthus, nerines and other slightly tender bulbous plants, hydrangeas, camellias, many of the smaller kinds of rhododendrons and azaleas especially if your garden soil is alkaline when these plants cannot be planted in the border, clipped bay and box and the slower-growing conifers.

Window boxes, which are available in wood, plastic or metal, must be very firmly secured. For a sash-type window the box can stand on the ledge, raised an inch or so on blocks so that the water can drain away freely. It should be held by bolts, metal straps or bars. For casement windows, boxes must be fixed a few inches below the ledge so that the windows can be opened over the top of the plants. Fasten with metal straps or support by brackets fixed to the wall.

The John Innes composts may be used but the lightweight peat composts may be better for window boxes. Use crocks if these are available to help the drainage [3] and then add a layer of roughage [4]. Plant with a trowel [5].

Aftercare is a matter of feeding, keeping a look-out for pests and diseases, removing faded flowers and, if the containers are not placed where they can receive sufficient rain, watering [6].

Rock Gardening

The fascination of rock plants is increasing as the size of the average garden decreases for it is possible to grow many of these delightful and varied plants in a small area. Rock plants are very diverse in character but they should all be small, compact, neat and slow growing. Although the main flowering period is in the spring, it is possible by choosing plants carefully to have something in flower for practically every week of the year. The rock garden specialist frowns on the use of annual and biennial plants and would not dream of using gazanias, mesembryanthemums, dwarf antirrhinums and other summer-flowering plants to fill the gaps but if such plants give us pleasure in our own gardens why not plant them.

Rock plants like an open, sunny position away from overhanging trees. Although they like plenty of moisture during the growing season, they do not like winter wet. In their mountain homes they are for months protected by a deep, crisp layer of snow which keeps the plants dry and at an even, if low, temperature. Unusual and favourite plants can be protected from excessive winter rains by small cloches or just a sheet of glass supported over the plant.

If you are new to rock gardening, I would suggest that you start by growing a few plants in pots and pans and then perhaps graduate to a trough. A rock bed will be easier to plant and maintain than a rock garden. Some rock plants can look charming planted between paving stones in a path and a dry wall built and planted with rock plants will be very attractive especially in a terraced garden. Where suitable stone is available locally it is far better and more economical to make use of it, rather than, for instance, transporting limestone from the Lake District to a Sussex garden where the local warm-looking sandstone would be much more in keeping with the surroundings. Stones with well-defined strata or lines are best, granite and marble being the most unsuitable types. A properly constructed rock garden should, as far as possible, look like a natural outcrop of rocks and give the impression that the rocks seen above the surface are far fewer than those that lie beneath. To give this impression it is not necessary to use enormous lumps of stone although if they are available one or two large pieces will provide the keystones around which the rock garden is built. The rocks should be laid so that the strata lines run in approximately the same direction.

Many of the smaller and more tender rock and alpine plants are particularly suited to growing in pots or pans [1] where they can be a tremendous source of interest. This is the best way of growing some of the more fragile plants as they can be protected from winter dampness and I think it is much easier to appreciate the delicate beauty of these tiny plants when they can be raised up.

Trough gardens These are a further step on from growing rock plants in pans and properly planted they can be a very ornamental feature, particularly effective on paved areas. The choice of container is important, it must provide a good foil to the plants. You may be lucky enough to find a suitable stone trough but one of the old stone sinks can be fairly easily adapted. The sink should first be cleaned and painted with a bonding adhesive. Then, make up a mixture of 1 part of cement, 3 parts of sand and 1 part of peat with sufficient water added to make a thick paste. This mixture is applied to the sink just as the adhesive is drying off. Press it on firmly, a little at a time, and leave the surface rough [2]. I have found that a mixture of cow manure, soot and clay painted over the outside of the finished trough will encourage the growth of moss.

Drainage must be especially good and there should always be a drainage hole in the container. This is one of the reasons why an old sink is so useful for this purpose as the plug hole provides a good outlet for excess water, but do remember not to cover it with cement. The drainage hole and bottom of the trough should be covered with some pieces of crock and rubble and then with a layer of peat or rotted leaves [3]. The next step is to fill the trough with compost and before deciding which compost to use it will be necessary to consider what plants are to go in the trough. Some, such as cassiope, andromeda and phyllodoce, are peat lovers, others are lime hating and for these the compost chosen must be a lime-free one. For the most part I use a mixture of 2 parts of peat, 1 part of soil and 1 part of sharp sand, and then make adjustments accordingly.

To supply adequate growing conditions the compost should have a depth of at least 4in. with a $\frac{1}{2}$in. space at the top for watering. Make the compost reasonably firm as you go [4], packing it well into the sides and corners and if small rocks are to be added, and I do think these enhance the effect, then position them before the trough is filled

and work the soil in around them. Remember, too, that the trough is primarily intended for growing plants and do not add too many rocks.

Planting can be done in the usual way using a small trowel [5] and the plants chosen should be those that take kindly to confined conditions. Some suitable ones include *Androsace sarmentosa*, *Armeria caespitosa*, *Campanula arvatica* and *C. cochlearifolia*, *Dianthus alpinus*, *Erinus alpinus*, *Phlox douglasii* and its varieties, the Kabschia saxifrages, *Sempervivum arachnoideum*. Tiny shrubs such as *Juniperus communis compressa* and a willow, *Salix arbuscula*, which grows only about 9in. tall, are also useful as they give some height. If the container is large enough then a few of the miniature spring-flowering bulbs may be added.

Finally, stone chippings can be sprinkled over the surface [6] to give a good finish as well as deterring weeds but be careful not to use limestone chippings on lime-hating plants.

Aftercare of sink gardens is very straightforward, occasional hand weeding and watering in dry weather being all that is required.

Building a rock garden The small pieces of stone I am seen handling here [1] are quite sufficient in size to form a pleasing rock garden. The rocks are being built into an existing bank and I am laying them to give the impression of natural lines or strata as mentioned in the introduction. For each piece of rock the soil must be dug out to form a shelf, which should slope slightly downwards into the bank. The rocks must be stable and to prevent wobbling the soil should be carefully packed behind and around each one [2]. This will also ensure that there are no air pockets into which roots may penetrate and die.

It is more difficult to build a natural looking rock garden on a flat area, all too often this deteriorates into a heap of stones. However, this can be achieved [3] but it will be necessary to have some larger, squarer stones to build the levels successfully and create a series of steps with plateaus and crevices to hold the plants. Take care to pack the soil well around the rocks so that there is no instability.

A rock garden is a natural adjunct to a garden pool, particularly as a border of slightly overhanging stones is one of the best ways to soften the hard outlines of a fibreglass or, as shown here [4], a cement pool. Heavy rocks need careful handling when being moved into position or injuries may easily be caused.

My own rock garden [5] is situated on the south-facing slope to the front of the house. The natural slope of the garden was a tremendous help in achieving the various levels required for planting, but if there is insufficient space in your garden for this, then a flat rock bed [6] can be an attractive alternative. And for a south- or west-facing corner which needs to be given additional interest the raised rock bed [7] is another suggestion. Rock beds can be planted up as suggested for trough gardens but do remember to make adequate provision for drainage with plenty of rough clinker, ash or rubble at the bottom.

Dry walls These are useful for separating one part of the garden from another or as retaining walls. When constructing them I think it is better to put a small amount of cement between the layers of stone [8] as this will keep weeding to a minimum. Retaining walls should have a slight backward slope both to provide better support and to allow rain to get to the plants. Earth should be packed in solidly behind them as they are built and some should be allowed to come through between the stones to make planting areas.

A dry wall can bring much additional colour to the garden when planted with a range of
rock plants to flower throughout the year

After the rock garden has been completed it is a good plan to topdress the soil. Where you are growing lime-hating plants peat makes a good topdressing [1]. In fact, peat can be used for all plants as it helps to retain moisture and is gradually absorbed into the soil to improve its consistency. If the natural soil is on the heavy side coarse sand can be worked in with a handfork. Where the natural soil is poor it is best to remove it and replace it with a prepared compost of fibrous soil, moist peat and coarse sand.

As rock plants are grown in pots in the nursery, it is safe to plant out pot-grown plants [2] at any time, even while they are in flower. Planting between rocks must be done carefully with a small trowel [3]. Make sure that the soil is firmed evenly and, if necessary, shade the plants for a day or two from strong sun. Do not plant too closely as many rock plants spread rapidly and if you have room to include some small conifers and shrubs these should be planted first.

There is such a wide range of rock plants that choosing which to grow is difficult. I suggest, as a start, a collection containing *Alyssum saxatile*, armerias, aubrietas, campanulas, the smaller

species and varieties of dianthus, geranium species, the low-growing helianthemums, iberis, alpine species of phlox; if you have peaty soil then various species of primula, such as *P. rosea, P. marginata, P. viallii*, would be a good choice. And no collection would be complete without some of the saxifrages, sedums, sempervivums and thymes. Lime-hating plants include the lithospermums, lewisias and their hybrids, and most of the autumn-flowering species of gentian.

Many of the small bulbous plants are also excellent for rock gardens, look out for dwarf narcissi and tulip species, anemones, camassias, cyclamen, fritillaries, eranthis, crocus, *Iris reticulata, Iris danfordiae*, ixias, leucojums and scillas.

When planting I like to make sure that each plant is placed in a pocket of good compost [4]. This is particularly important when planting up walls and adequate space should be left when building them to allow for this. When choosing the plants for a dry wall or near vertical rock garden you will find that the mat-forming and trailing ones such as the aethionemas, alyssums, androsaces, arabis, aubrietas, campanulas, lithospermums, phlox,

saxifrages and sempervivums will be particularly spectacular.

Rock plants can also be grown in paving or in steps which connect one garden level with another. Once again, the choice of plants for this purpose is wide and includes aubrietas, alyssums, campanulas, erinus, geranium species, saxifrages, sedums, sempervivums and thymes. Holes can be left for plants when the steps are built but if this was overlooked it is not difficult to make holes large enough for the plants with a hammer and cold chisel [5].

It is worth going over rock garden plants quite frequently to cut off dead flowers [6], and in autumn any dead leaves, which may collect in the crevices between rocks, should be removed regularly otherwise they get wet and soggy and kill the plants they are covering.

Many of the rock plants dislike winter dampness and this is the most frequent cause of death, particularly of the rather delicate lewisias and those, such as the edelweiss, which have hairy leaves. These plants survive cold damp winters better if they are protected with a pane of glass which can be supported over them on four short sticks and kept in place with a stone, or a cloche may be used.

Water Gardening

A garden pool, no matter how small, can be one of the most attractive features in the garden. When planning the garden it is most important to work all the features in with the general plan and with this in mind the geometrically shaped pools – round, square, rectangular – are only at home in the formal garden. With an informal garden, and this is the kind I have, the pool should have a fluid outline which will enable it to blend in with the rest of the garden.

The site is the next important consideration. Most water plants enjoy sunshine, so the pool should be placed in an open position well away from any trees. I like to see a pool made with various depths to accommodate the requirements of both fish and plants, a maximum depth of 18 in. to 2 ft. will be suitable for a range of water lilies, with shelves 3 to 6 in. deep for marginal plants. When deciding on the depth do remember to keep the pool shallow if you have small children to whom it might be a danger.

There are various ways of making pools and these differ in cost and other factors. The traditional way is by using concrete. This gives a solid and hardwearing surface but concrete pools take rather longer to construct than pools made from one or other of the plastics. Several types of flexible plastic pool liners are available of which the polythene sheeting is the cheapest but is not so durable as the PVC or the butyl rubber kinds. They are an easy way of making a pool but you should remember that they will lose their effectiveness if punctured in any way, as patching is not often very successful. The rigid fibreglass pools are more expensive than the flexible types but are durable and extremely easy to install.

Whichever type of pool you decide on its ornamental value will depend on maintaining the correct balance of plants, fish and snails to prevent it from becoming stagnant. The pool itself should be planted with some of the flowering aquatics and oxygenating plants (page 70) and almost equally important is the choice of marginal and waterside plants which play such a large part in concealing the edges of the pool. A selection of plants for growing in moist soil or in up to 3 in. of water includes the sweet flag, the flowering rush, the marsh marigold, irises, especially *I. kaempferi* and *I. laevigata*, the pickerel weed, bulrushes and the reed mace.

Good plants for a moist position above water level include astilbe, hostas, ferns, mimulus and primulas.

Concrete pools The best time to start the construction of a concrete pool is in the autumn but it is important not to attempt the work in frosty weather. First, excavate the hole to the size and shape you have planned. I find it is much easier to have the sides sloping gently to the bottom and the maximum depth need only be from 2 to 2½ ft. This will allow for a thickness of 6 in. of concrete on the bottom and leave a final pool depth of 1½ to 2 ft. at the deepest point. The next part of the procedure, and this really is important, is to get the surrounds of the pool perfectly level. Water always finds its own level and if the pool has a slope you will have one end full while a lot of edge will be showing at the other end. To check the level you will need a number of pegs, a fairly long piece of plank and a spirit level. First, hammer the pegs into the ground at intervals around the sides of your excavated hole [1]. One peg should act as the marker peg and be set so that its top is at the desired level of the pool sides. Then, place the plank across the tips of the marker peg and the nearest adjacent peg [2] and check with the spirit level [3]. Continue doing this between all the pegs, adjusting them if necessary [4] until all the tops are lined up to that of the marker peg. The tops of the pegs will then indicate the finished height of the sides of the pool, which is now ready to be concreted. The ideal mixture to use should be made up of 3 parts of gravel, 2 of sand and 1 of cement. Do not mix up too much at a time and if the work is being done in hot weather then keep the finished work covered with wet sacks to prevent too rapid drying. The sides of the pool are made first and the concrete should be thick enough to withstand any freezing and expansion of water. Once concrete cracks it is almost impossible to repair it properly. I used a thickness of 4 in. on the sides and slope of my pool and finished by trowelling off to get a smooth surface on the slope [5]. When the sides are complete, the finished level of concrete should line up with the tops of the levelling pegs [6]. Concrete should be put in the bottom of the pool to a depth of 6 in. and left for a week to harden.

Fill the pool with water and leave it for at least three weeks then remove this water and put in fresh before adding plants or fish.

When the pool is finished, the edges should be hidden by placing rocks around the sides [7] and by a careful choice of planting material such as this prostrate juniper [8].

Modern fibreglass pools and the use of plastic liners have made the job of constructing a water garden much easier.

Fibreglass pools These are available in a wide range of shapes and sizes. All are made with shelves [1] to accommodate the various types of pool plants and are simplicity itself to install. Mark out the shape of the pool in the desired position and excavate the soil to the various depths then try the pool for size and remove or add soil as necessary. Put the pool in position, packing any gaps with sand and check that the top is level with a spirit level. As with concrete pools it is most important to soften and hide the edge of the pool with plants or stones.

Pool liners Though there are several types of pool liner the initial preparation is the same for all. First, mark out the shape and size of the pool. Then dig the hole, taking care to keep the bottom and sides level. Next, and this is especially important, remove all stones or pebbles from the bottom and sides, otherwise these will easily puncture the plastic or rubber, and cover the bottom with a layer of sand to give a smooth base [2].

The liner is placed in position, the edges are anchored with flat stones and the pool is filled with water [3]. As with the fibreglass pools the edges of the liner should be concealed [4].

When selecting which liner to use there are certain factors which will affect your decision. The polythene sheet is the cheapest and the most economical though it may be necessary to use a double thickness for a larger pool. PVC is more durable and more expensive but the toughened butyl rubber [5] is really the best for its length of life and for the way it takes the contours of the pool without wrinkling.

Fountains and waterfalls One of the added pleasures of a water garden is to have some movement of the water and this will also improve oxygenation, but for plants such as water lilies it is important that any water movement is very slow. In order to install a pump and/or fountain [6] you will need to have a handy electric point to supply the power and all the equipment must be properly insulated. If in doubt I advise that you consult an electrician and get him to do the job for you.

I use a submersible pump in my own pool. These are effective and reliable and are easy to install.

Planting This is usually done when the pool is empty or half full and the best time is from the end of May to early August. There are several methods of planting water lilies, one is to put a 6-in. layer of soil over the floor and plant in this but there are disadvantages as the plants are not so easily controlled, cleaning is difficult and the fish constantly stir the soil up and make the water muddy. Another way is to make a special bed on the bottom of the pool. Pieces of stone can be used [1] to make the bed which is filled with good fibrous soil, some chopped turf if possible and a handful of bonemeal and the plant is set in this [2]. A few stones over the top will hold the soil and plant in place. But the handiest method is to use the plastic planting baskets sold especially for this purpose. Put a layer of the compost previously described around the sides and bottom of the basket and set the plant in this [3]. The compost should be packed firmly around the roots [4] and a layer of gravel over the surface will prevent disturbance by fish. The basket is then placed on the floor of the pool. One considerable advantage of this method is that it is very easy to renew the soil when required, usually every three or four years, simply by lifting out

the baskets and replacing the soil with fresh. Less elaborate planting is needed for such oxygenating plants as elodea. These plants absorb most of their food from the water and their roots act more or less as an anchorage only. A rubber band placed round the root ball [5] is sufficient to hold it together and it can then be put on the floor of the pool.

The marginal plants only require a covering of about 3 to 4 in. of water. They are planted in the same way as just described, either in specially prepared beds of soil and stones or in smaller versions of the planting baskets.

When filling the pool, run the water in gently from a hose [6]. Another advantage of planting in baskets is that the pool can be filled with water before planting and this will give it time to warm up before any plants are added. Do not introduce fish to the pool until the plants have had a chance to settle in – a few weeks should be sufficient.

Choosing the plants I think that water lilies will be most people's first choice. Varieties are available for growing in depths ranging from 12 in. to 3 ft. Excellent kinds for pools of medium depth, $1\frac{1}{2}$ to 2 ft. or so, include the red James Brydon, the yellow *Nymphaea odorata sulphurea* and the varieties of *N.*

marliacea in white, pale and deep pink, red and yellow. For shallower pools, up to 12 in., the varieties of *N. laydekeri* are good and they are in a range of colours – white, lilac, pink, deep red – also the white *N. pygmaea alba* with star-like flowers and its pale yellow counterpart *N. pygmaea helvola*.

But in addition to the water lilies there are other aquatics with floating flowers or foliage which should not be overlooked. These include the water hawthorn, *Aponogeton distachyus*, white strongly scented flowers; water violet, *Hottonia palustris*, white or lavender flowers; *Villarsia nymphaeoides*, bright yellow fringed flowers; and floating plants such as water soldier *Stratiotes aloides* with white flowers and frog-bit, *Hydrocharis morsus-ranae*, also with white flowers.

Then if you are intending to have fish in the pool you should have some oxygenating plants, elodea is one of the best known, others include potamogeton and the milfoil, *Myriophyllum spicatum*. The water violet is also good for this purpose.

Marginal plants are given on page 67.

Pool maintenance Provided the correct balance of plants, fish and snails is maintained most pools require the minimum of routine care. It is important, however, to remove regularly any dead leaves and other debris and for this I use a wire rake [1].

After six years I found it necessary to remove some plants because of overcrowding. In particular, these bulrushes [2] have proved to be too vigorous. Other plants, too, will need dividing every few years and this can be combined with a general spring cleaning.

Before emptying and cleaning the pool, you must catch the fish [3] and put them in temporary alternative accommodation, and I think this is a good point to say something about fish for the garden pool. First, when you are thinking about stocking the pool you should calculate the number of fish to have by allowing a 3-in. length of fish for every square foot of surface area. It is most important not to overcrowd them as this will lead to disease and will not allow the fish sufficient space to develop or, indeed, enough naturally occurring food. Of course, it is easy to supplement the food but in a well-balanced, properly planted pool this should not be necessary and do remember that overfeeding can kill. Unless the pool is less than 15 in. deep, the fish require no protection in winter. However, if the water freezes over and remains frozen for over a week it is necessary to bore a hole about 6 in. in diameter in the ice to allow any gas given off by decaying matter in the pool to escape. Take care when making the hole not to break the ice with heavy blows as this may injure or kill the fish.

There are several types of fish which are hardy and can be allowed to mix freely. These include the lovely golden and silver orfe, the shubunkins in a mixture of colours – red, white, black, silver, yellow and blue, goldfish and comet longtails.

Once the fish have been removed, the water can be siphoned out [4], this will be quicker than bucketing and while it is proceeding you can start lifting the plants. Here [5] I am removing a large iris. It is six years since my pool was established and among the plants which have become too large are the water lilies, some having grown to such an extent that I had to chop them into pieces to get them out [6]. Finally, the bottom of the pool is hosed [7] and scrubbed down [8] to remove all traces of scum and debris.

Chrysanthemums and Dahlias

Few flowers add so much colour to the late summer and autumn garden as the chrysanthemums and there are not many flowers that are so valuable for garden display and for cutting for the house. The outdoor chrysanthemums are the early flowerers and these are grown in the open ground without any protection. As they finish flowering the greenhouse varieties will be starting and these will carry on until well after Christmas.

The chrysanthemum is a very variable flower and the various types have been classified according to the shape and formation of the flowers. For garden display, it is the quantity rather than the size of the bloom that really matters. I would recommend the Singles which have daisy flowers with distinct yellow centres; the Anemones which are similar to the Singles but these have a cushion centre of short florets; the Pompons with very small fully double flowers like buttons; the Koreans which are single or double flowered; the Sprays which have small double or single flowers borne in clusters, and the Charm and Cascade groups which have small single flowers freely produced in sprays. The Exhibition and Decorative classes are better grown in the greenhouse. These have large, fully double flowers.

Dahlias are splendid border flowers for they have a very long flowering season lasting from mid-summer right through until the frosts come in autumn. They, too, make excellent cut flowers. Dahlias can be a valuable addition to the mixed border, they look very striking when grown in a bed on their own and the dwarf varieties are among my favourite bedding plants. Dahlias are also divided into groups according to the shape and formation of their flowers like the chrysanthemum. Again I would advise growing the medium and small-flowered varieties for garden display reserving the large-flowered types for exhibition work. The Cactus and Semi-cactus dahlias have spiky flowers and the flatter-petalled types are called Decoratives. Dahlias with globular flowers less than 2in. in diameter are called Pompons and above this size are called Ball dahlias. The dwarf dahlias, up to about 2ft. in height, are the bedding dahlias.

A good catalogue will offer you a wide choice of both dahlias and chrysanthemums in a wide and beautiful colour range.

CHRYSANTHEMUMS

Propagation from cuttings In the initial stages this is the same procedure for both greenhouse and outdoor varieties. The stools of both kinds of chrysanthemum, which have been boxed up as I shall describe later, will produce short sturdy growths from their bases [1] and it is these growths which provide the cuttings. Cuttings of outdoor kinds are best taken between mid-February and the end of March and those of indoor kinds between late February and early March. When making the cuttings choose sturdy shoots springing directly from the roots [2] and after removing the bottom leaves trim the shoots just below a joint using a sharp knife [3]. Dip the ends in hormone-rooting powder and insert them in $3\frac{1}{2}$-in. pots containing John Innes seed compost [4]. I usually put about six cuttings in a pot and it is important that each cutting should be well firmed in. After the cuttings have been inserted, label the pots and give them a good watering. If possible, place the pots in a propagating case as this encourages rapid rooting, but if this is not available then keep them in a temperature of 10 to 16°C. (50 to 60°F.).

Once they have made some growth [5] the rooted cuttings are potted on into individual $3\frac{1}{2}$-in. pots [6] and for this potting I use John Innes No. 1 potting compost.

Greenhouse chrysanthemums Once the small plants are well established in the $3\frac{1}{2}$-in. pots, and this is usually about mid-April, they are transferred to 5-in. pots [7] and when well established in these, the end of May or early June, they are potted finally into 8 or 9-in. ones. For the final potting I use John Innes No. 2 compost. Firm potting is necessary to get the best results from chrysanthemums and a wooden potting stick [8] makes this easier. When doing this potting I like to leave about 2in. between the soil surface and the top of the pot to allow room for a topdressing of compost in August or early September.

Staking This may be necessary from the time the plants are in their first pots and in this case a thin bamboo cane will be all that is needed. After they are in their final pots a strong cane should be used for support to prevent the stems being broken off by the wind. Some gardeners use three or four canes placed around the outside of each plant but this is mainly required for exhibition blooms. Do not tie the stems too tightly to the canes as it is important to leave room for growth.

Stopping The reason for stopping is to encourage the plant to form shoots and flower buds earlier than it would naturally. All that is involved is the removal of the growing tips by pinching them out with the finger and thumb [1]. The greenhouse varieties are stopped first in March or April with a second stop in June or early July. Most catalogues give the stopping dates for each variety.

Summer standing ground From June to September the chrysanthemums are moved to an area out of doors. Ideally, the standing ground should be covered with ash [2] or concrete or the pots should be stood on slates or tiles. This will prevent worms entering the pots and damaging the root systems. Position the pots in double rows allowing 18 in. between the plants and 3 ft. between the double rows. At each end of the row a stake should be inserted and a wire stretched between the two. The canes in the pots can then be attached to the wire which will stop the plants from being blown over.

During the summer the plants may need watering several times a day and I like to feed the plants about once a fortnight from early August using either a liquid or a dry fertilizer [3] but the dry one must be well watered in. Choose either a general fertilizer or one of the proprietary chrysanthemum ones.

Thinning and disbudding Thinning simply means the removal of the side shoots which grow from the leaf axils. Nip these out when they are about 1 to 1½ in. long [4] and do this down the whole length of the stem, leaving 8 to 10 shoots in all on each plant.

Disbudding is done as soon as the buds are large enough to snap out [5]. I usually make a start in early August with the large exhibition varieties and carry on into early October when the decoratives and singles are disbudded. The centre bud is retained and all the surrounding ones pinched out.

Housing the plants The greenhouse chrysanthemums must be brought into the house before the frosts begin. Before housing the plants, spray them with an insecticide and fungicide to kill any pests and diseases [6]. One point to remember is to carry the plants into the house pot first. This reduces the danger of breaking off shoots. Continue to feed the plants until flower production is well under way [7] and keep the plants watered [8].

After flowering, cut the stems back to within 9 in. of the compost and box the stools as shown on page 76. The boxes are kept in the greenhouse until shoots are produced.

Outdoor chrysanthemums The rooted cuttings are potted on into 3½-in. pots, hardened off in a frame and, when a good root system has been formed [1], planted out in late April or early May. Prepare the ground beforehand, digging it deeply and incorporating some well-rotted manure or compost. The plants should be set out 1½ to 2 ft. apart in rows 3 ft. apart and the stakes should be placed in position first. Then, knock the plants gently out of their pots and plant with a trowel [2]. Do not plant too deeply but firm the plants in really well. The plants should be placed close to the stakes and the stems tied to these after planting to stop them from being broken off.

Stop the plants about mid-May by pinching out the centre growing point of each [3]. This will cause the plant to branch and as new growths develop they should be tied into the support. One stopping is usually sufficient for outdoor kinds. From July onwards I feed the plants with a general or special chrysanthemum fertilizer. Scatter this round the plants [4], hoe it in and water thoroughly. Soluble fertilizer dissolved in water can also be used.

As the plants grow you will need to check regularly and tie in all new growth to prevent wind damage. By late July it will be necessary to disbud, unless you are growing the plants to provide sprays of flowers. If large flowers are required, or if they are needed for exhibition, I leave one flower bud, the central or crown bud, to each stem [5] and remove all the surrounding buds. It is safer to leave the buds until they can be handled easily, premature disbudding may result in damage to the crown bud. At the same time, remove any side shoots which are forming in the leaf axils in order to divert all the plants' energy into producing good blooms with long stems.

As the flowers develop they will need some protection from the damaging effects of wind and rain. Transparent greaseproof bags [6] are ideal for this.

When the flowers are over the plants can be cut down to a few inches from ground level [7]. Make sure they are labelled properly. Then in mid-November lift the roots, or stools as they are often called, and put them in boxes covering the roots with sand or peat [8]. In the case of outdoor chrysanthemums, the boxes of stools should be kept in a frostproof shed or cellar until they are needed for cuttings, when they should be transferred to a heated greenhouse to encourage shoots to grow.

DAHLIAS

From cuttings Dahlias are usually propagated from cuttings which are made from the young shoots produced by the boxed up tubers. When the young shoots are about 3 in. long each one should be cut off [1] together with a small portion of the old stem, which is called a heel [2]. Trim the bases of the cuttings to remove any ragged edges and trim off the bottom pair of leaves. When the cuttings have been prepared, the ends can be dipped in hormone-rooting powder as this will aid rapid root formation. The cuttings can then be inserted into boxes or pots of John Innes seed compost, and for this job I like to use a wooden dibber. After watering the containers they should be placed on the greenhouse staging and covered with sheets of newspaper for a few days to protect them from the sun and to prevent flagging [3]. If possible, a temperature of at least 13°C. (55°F.) should be maintained. Mist propagators or a closed propagating frame can also be used. Make sure that you keep each variety separate and labelled.

When the cuttings start to grow they can be potted on individually into 3½-in. pots of John Innes No. 1 compost. If the cuttings were taken early in the year they may need to be repotted into 5-in. pots [4,5], otherwise they will become short of food before they are planted out.

Before the young plants can be placed out in the garden they must be acclimatized gradually to lower temperatures – a procedure known as hardening off. Put the pots in a cold frame in early May, or mid-May in colder areas, and increase the amount of ventilation gradually until the lights are left off altogether [6]. Do not forget to check the plants regularly in case they need watering.

Planting out To do well, dahlias need a deep, rich well-dug soil containing plenty of organic matter such as garden compost or rotted manure and before planting I give the soil a dressing of general fertilizer at 2 to 3 oz. to the sq. yd.

The planting time is very important and depends on the part of the country in which one lives. Rooted cuttings can be planted out in mid-May in the South, but it is advisable to wait until early June in the North. I use a hand trowel for pot-grown plants and make a hole [7] which will allow the root ball to be set so that its top is only about half an inch below soil level.

Insert the stake before planting, put the plant in position and return the soil around the roots, firming well [8].

From tubers For gardeners who do not have a greenhouse or who do not wish to go to the trouble of taking cuttings, dahlia plants can be grown directly from tubers. These are stored throughout the winter, as described on page 79, and then can be planted in the garden in late April or early May. Insert the stakes before planting (if pushed in afterwards they may damage the tubers) and use a spade or trowel, depending on the size of the tubers, to make the hole. Place the dormant tubers about 3 to 4 in. deep [1] and firm the soil well around them. When planting do not forget that the taller growing varieties need a minimum distance of 3 ft. between plants, the smaller bedding types a minimum of 1½ ft.

If the roots are large it is possible to split them up into a number of smaller ones before planting [2]. When doing this it is important that each division should consist of a stem with a tuber or tubers attached.

Once the dormant tubers start to grow they will produce a number of shoots and to prevent overcrowding, which causes drawn, thin shoots, I remove all the surplus ones [3] leaving about three strong shoots to each plant.

Care after planting When dahlia plants reach about 8 to 9 in. in height, it is a good idea to pinch out the main growing points [4]. This will encourage the side shoots to grow and will result in a bushy plant with a larger number of flowers.

After planting and throughout the growing season dahlias need plenty of water and, to conserve soil moisture, the area around the plants can be mulched. A 2 to 3-in. layer of straw, peat, garden compost or rotted manure can be used, but if you are growing plants for exhibition then try to mulch with manure.

Dahlias grow rapidly from May onwards and they should be fed regularly with a general fertilizer. This is sprinkled around the plants and watered in [5]. If you have mulched the ground then scrape the mulch away first.

I have already mentioned briefly the use of stakes. Dahlias are leafy plants and their stout hollow branches are easily damaged by wind, so it is necessary to make sure that the plants are well supported. This is especially true of the tall varieties which need good strong stakes, preferably of 1-in. square wood. Such stakes should be treated with a wood preservative, which is harmless to plants, before use. If I use bamboo canes to provide support, I prefer to put one in when I am planting and then when the plants are growing to put three or four more around each plant [6].

Disbudding Some disbudding may be necessary, although I do not bother about this with the small-flowered varieties used for garden decoration as, in this case, masses of flowers are wanted to provide a good display. With large-flowered kinds and those needed for exhibition, except small pompons where large flowers are not required, it is necessary to remove a fairly large proportion of the buds. The flower buds form at the top of each shoot or stem and it is the lower ones which should be pinched out, using the fingers and thumb [1], so that only the bud at the apex of the shoot – the crown bud – is left [2]. The buds should be removed when they are fairly small.

Side shooting By late July or August it will also be necessary to thin out some of the surplus young side shoots higher up the plant, otherwise it becomes a mass of foliage with poor quality flowers. This is done by snapping off all the side shoots for about 1½ to 2 ft. from the tip of each stem. The shoots lower down the plant are left to grow and provide replacement stems to flower later. Gardeners who are growing dahlias for exhibition or who require them specially for cutting usually start this thinning much earlier and continue to do it at

regular intervals. But for good general garden displays I do not think that it is an important job.

Cutting down and lifting When frost threatens in early autumn go over the plants and pick all the remaining flowers. Before cutting down and lifting the plants I tie a label to the base of the stem of each one. This label should give details of the variety, colour, height and type for easy identification in the spring. If you do not know the name of the variety you can still add the other details and these will help you to plan colour combinations for the following year. The stems should be cut down to within 9 to 12 in. of the ground and it is best to use a pair of secateurs to do this job as the stems are usually quite tough by this time of year [3].

The tubers should be lifted with a garden fork [4] and this needs to be done carefully so that they are not damaged in any way, so work well away from the stems.

Drying and storing As soon as the tuberous roots are lifted they should be dried off in a frostproof place. First, remove any soil, then cut away damaged parts of the tubers and dust the cut surfaces with a powder made up from equal parts of ground limestone and

flowers of sulphur. After this I dry them off by placing the roots upside down between strips of wood nailed across the opening of a wooden box [5]. They are left in this position for three or four weeks to allow any moisture or sap to drain from the stems. When the tubers have dried off they are either placed in dry peat in boxes or wrapped in newspaper and stored in a frostproof place such as an attic, cellar or garage. Check the tubers occasionally during the winter to see if any fungus is forming and, if it is, dust them with flowers of sulphur.

From February onwards, tubers intended for the production of cuttings can be taken out of store and started into growth. To do this they are placed on layers of peat in seed boxes and then covered with more peat [6]. Keep them moist and in a temperature of about 10°C. (50°F.). This encourages the dormant buds on the tubers to start sprouting and it is these sprouts which provide the cuttings.

The remaining tubers can be left in store until planting time in late April or early May.

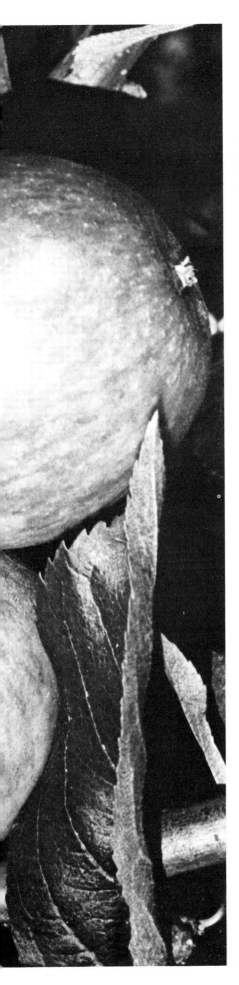

Fruit Growing

No well-planned garden is complete without a section devoted to fruit, however small it is, and there are many often surprising places where a fruit bush or tree can be fitted in. Why not consider having an apple or pear tree as a specimen planting on a lawn? These can be very attractive with their lovely blossom in the spring and handsome fruit in the autumn.

Apple and pear varieties which have been grafted on to dwarfing rootstocks may be trained in cordon and espalier form to make a decorative fruit hedge which will make an excellent screen to the vegetable garden. Walls and fences will provide opportunities to grow trained fruit trees especially fan-shaped specimens. Peaches will benefit from the shelter and extra warmth gained from a south or west-facing wall and Morello cherries do very well on north-facing walls. Pears, plums and even apples will also respond well to this treatment.

Soft fruits are economically sound for a small garden for they take up relatively little space and give very good crops. I personally would give priority to raspberries for a ten-yard row will provide an average family with sufficient fruit throughout June and into late July when it is really appreciated. They are also excellent for deep freezing. Blackcurrants are comparatively easy to grow, relatively trouble free and they crop well. Strawberries are, of course, always popular but they are not a permanent crop for the plants should be renewed at least every three years. Gooseberries are popular in certain districts and red and white currants will give good returns though they are less widely grown.

Commercial establishments grow varieties which are proven good croppers and which have a saleable appearance but this is often at the expense of flavour. Home growers should therefore try to choose varieties which are known to be good for flavour even if they are not so productive or so good looking.

Apples The most suitable forms of apple tree for a small garden are the single-stemmed cordon and the espalier, both of which are trained to horizontal wires strained from strong posts, and the bush and dwarf pyramid which are grown in the open. The most suitable varieties are those grafted on to dwarfing rootstocks. The rootstock known as Malling IX or 106 is very dwarfing but if the soil is poor the semi-dwarfing Malling II will be needed. Trees on the stock M.26 do not need staking and MM.106 is another good dwarfing stock.

When ordering apple varieties remember that very few are self-fertile and all will be better for the presence of a suitable cross-pollinating variety. The lack of a pollinator is often the reason why fruit trees do not bear any fruit and it is always best to consult the nurseryman about this when ordering your trees.

Good varieties for a small garden include Cox's Orange Pippin and James Grieve which is a good pollinator for the Cox. Other eating apples which I would recommend are Ellison's Orange, Lord Lambourne and Laxton's Superb. The best cooking apple for a small or medium-sized garden is Lane's Prince

Albert. Bramley Seedling is a popular variety for a larger tree and Newton Wonder is delicious for eating and cooking.

Apples will grow in almost any reasonably good garden soil although the best results are obtained in a rather deep soil with good drainage. A sunny, sheltered site is the best. The soil should be prepared very thoroughly by digging or forking well and working in rotted manure or garden compost at the rate of 1 cwt. to 15 sq. yd. A topdressing of a good compound fertilizer should be given at the rate of 3 to 4 oz. per sq. yd. before planting. Apples can be planted between November and March if the trees are lifted from the open ground or at any time of the year if they are purchased in containers.

Fruit trees, and other ornamental trees and shrubs as well, often arrive from the nurseryman during bad weather or when you do not have time to plant. If this is the case leave them in their wrappings in a frost-free place for a few days until conditions improve. If bad weather is persistent take out a trench, lay the trees in at an angle and cover the roots with soil [1]. This process is known as heeling in and the plants will be perfectly safe until planting can take place.

The planting method for bush and dwarf pyramid trees is the same as described for trees and shrubs and the trees should be staked as shown [2,3,4]. Cordons are planted at an angle of 45 degrees [5] and both cordons and espaliers, which are planted upright, are trained to taut wires. The recommended planting distances are bush trees, 8 to 10 ft. apart; dwarf pyramids, 4 to 6 ft. apart; espalier trees, 12 to 15 ft. apart and single-stemmed cordons, 3 ft. apart.

It is important to plant to the correct depth – a good guide being the old soil mark on the stem which indicates the depth at which the plant was growing in the nursery. It is essential to keep the union of stock and scion above ground in grafted plants. Otherwise the scion will throw out roots and the benefit of the rootstock will be lost.

The trees can be protected against attacks by rabbits and hares with wire netting [6] or black polythene up to a height of about 4 ft.

Carry out routine spraying with one or two fungicides or pesticides to keep at bay those pests and diseases of apples which are most common. In winter when the trees are dormant spray them thoroughly with a tar-oil winter wash.

A pool will add a new dimension to the garden scene and the interest will be heightened if
fish, and even frogs, are introduced

This will kill the eggs of many overwintering pests and at the same time get rid of lichen and moss. In spring spraying with BHC at the green cluster stage will control caterpillars, winter moth, aphids, apple capsid, apple sucker and scale insects. A further spraying with BHC in May at petal fall should be effective against apple sawfly and another in June will kill codling moth. Look out for red spider mite in mid-June and if you spot it spray with a summer ovicide. For mildew use a lime-sulphur spray or dinocap on sulphur-shy varieties. Fruit trees should not be sprayed when they are flowering or the bees and other pollinating insects will be killed.

Each year dress the soil with a general fertilizer applied at the rate recommended by the manufacturer and then mulch the trees with organic matter. As the shoots of the trained trees develop during the spring and early summer tie these in. A bamboo cane fastened to the supporting wires to follow the same direction as cordon trees provides added support [1].

Apples to be stored should not be picked before they are mature when the pips will turn brown and only healthy fruit should be chosen. They can be placed on slatted shelves or trays in tiers

so that they can breathe. They will generate carbon dioxide which builds up and helps to preserve them. You can wrap them individually in oiled paper [2] and place them on shelves. Always store in a cool moist atmosphere.

PRUNING New apple trees should be pruned immediately after they have been planted. All the young stems should be shortened by about one third to one half and each cut should be made just above a growth bud which points away from the centre in bush trees [3] or in the direction in which the new growth is to be encouraged in espalier and cordon trees [4]. It is quite easy to tell the young growth from that which is older because the young growth has a smoother bark and it bears only growth buds which are small buds set very close to the stem. Older growth has darker, rougher bark and it may also have some fruit buds which are larger, rounder and stand out more prominently than the growth buds. Fruit buds may also grow in clusters on short-branched outgrowths known as spurs.

While the trees are becoming established during the first few years, continue to prune as in the first year but shorten some of the thinner side growths that are not required to make main

branches or stems to about 1 or 2 in. This will encourage them to form fruit buds and eventually spurs. As bush trees mature they will require less and less pruning eventually only needing the old and overcrowded branches, stems and spurs to be thinned out in autumn and winter.

Espaliers and cordons require more restrictive pruning. In July and August when the current year's growth is about the thickness of a pencil at the base and beginning to get woody, shorten each side shoot growing direct from the main stem or branch to four leaves, not counting the rosette of partly developed leaves which cluster around the base of most young shoots [5]. Continue to do this, a little at a time but do no pruning of this kind after mid-August. In November shorten the main stems by about one third and shorten the laterals to within two or three dormant buds of the main stem to encourage the production of fruiting spurs. Remove any sucker growths.

Some natural thinning of the fruit occurs and there is often quite a heavy drop of fruit towards the end of June. However, a further hand thinning may be necessary in July to leave two fruits at each spur [6].

Pears Pears are treated in a similar way to apples with regard to planting and general cultivation. They do better if given a rather warmer and more sheltered site than apples and need a slightly lighter soil for they resent cold, wet conditions. The choicest varieties should, for preference, be trained against a sunny wall or fence but there are many kinds which can be grown quite satisfactorily in the open as bushes. Trained trees are usually grown as cordons [1] or espaliers [2] and they are also successful as fan-trained specimens.

Like apples, pears are grown by nurserymen on stocks. For small bushes, espaliers and fan-shaped trees, varieties grafted on to Malling B are required and for single-stemmed cordons I would recommend Malling C.

Pears may be wholly or partly self-sterile and it is therefore wise to avoid planting varieties singly. Good varieties include Williams' Bon Cretien, Conference and Doyenne du Comice. Catillac is a good cooker.

A dressing of a slow-acting nitrogenous fertilizer such as hoof and horn or dried blood will be beneficial if applied in the spring and this should be followed by a mulch [3].

Pears are pruned in much the same way as apples. They do, however, form spurs very readily and so are especially suitable for growing as trained trees.

These are pruned in the summer shortening the laterals a few at a time during July and early August to five leaves [4]. During the winter the laterals may be further shortened to two buds each, the leading growths being cut back by about a third. Although the fruits may require some thinning this should not be done too drastically as some will fall when they are fully grown.

Fruit to be stored should be picked just before it is fully ripe. Each pear should be held lightly and should come away after being given a slight twist [5]. They are stored in a similar way to apples although some believe that they are best when left unwrapped.

The spraying programme for pears is similar to that for apples but watch out, too, for pear leaf blister mite which feeds on the tissue of the leaves and produces greenish-yellow blisters which turn red on the upper surface and the small white, maggot-like larvae of the pear midge which hatch from eggs laid in the flowers when they feed on the developing fruitlets. These become severely distorted and mis-shapen and rot and fall before they are fully

developed. Both these pests will be kept at bay if a regular spraying programme is maintained [6]. The manufacturer's instructions regarding the preparation and application of chemicals should be strictly adhered to. Try to carry out any spraying on a clear, still day.

Plums Plums make large trees very quickly and so they are not suitable for small gardens when grown in the open. However, they can be fan trained against a wall. They like fairly rich soils which are well supplied with lime and which do not get waterlogged in the winter. The best time for planting is November but it can be done at any time during the winter until March provided the weather is good.

Plum varieties are budded or grafted on to rootstocks. Common Plum and Pershore are suitable for fan-shaped trees. Good varieties are Czar, Early Transparent Gage, Victoria [1], Pershore and Monarch, all of which are self-fertile.

Here I am planting a five-year-old tree [2,3,4,5] and although this may be considered rather old, plums are sometimes slow in coming into bearing and if you plant a maiden tree it may be five or six years before any fruit is gathered. However, careful attention should be given to the aftercare of such a tree and it is best to plant in November so that the tree has a chance to become established before the summer. Plums are surface rooting and must not be planted too deeply. The union of stock and scion must be above soil level so the

planting holes should be shallow and wide.

Feed plums with a well-balanced general fertilizer every February and mulch with organic matter each spring. Plums are inclined to throw suckers and these should be pulled off at the roots. Thin plums to 2 in. apart when they have finished stoning, doing this over a period of about a week [6]. This thinning helps to check the biennial bearing for which plums are notorious.

Pruning should be carried out in late summer after the fruit has been picked. It should not be done during the winter as silver leaf disease may enter through wounds made in the winter. For this reason any large wounds made during pruning must be painted with Stockholm tar or like material. The unwanted side shoots in a fan-trained tree should be cut back to two dormant buds from the main branch but where possible young laterals should be trained in at practically full length.

Watch out for bacterial canker and brown rot (page 88) and also silver leaf disease (page 89). Birds may be a problem, too, and fan-trained trees can be netted. Sometimes a gum exudes from the fruit and this is a physiological condition and not a disease. There is no

very satisfactory control for this trouble although an application of Bordeaux mixture just before leaf fall may prove helpful.

The summer flower border is incomplete without a selection of dahlias. This is the small-flowered Cactus variety Salmon Rays

Cherries For a small garden, I would only consider growing the sour, cooking cherries as these are well adapted for training against a wall. The best of these are the Morello cherries [1] because they are self-fertile. They like a fairly rich loamy soil which is well supplied with lime.

They should be planted between November and March in a partially shaded position and they are ideal for a north-facing wall. Fan-shaped trees are planted 15 to 20 ft. apart against a wall which is at least 10 ft. high. Cherries are propagated by budding or grafting on to suitable rootstocks. The most commonly used is the Gean or wild cherry which is also known as the Mazzard. This is a vigorous stock but it has to serve for all purposes as no thoroughly satisfactory dwarfing stock has been found.

The planting holes for cherries should be wide and relatively shallow. This is because they make a spreading root system. The uppermost roots should be covered with 3 to 4 in. of soil. Cherries should be mulched in the spring after feeding with sulphate of potash at 4 to 6 oz. per tree [2]. Occasional dressings of Nitro-chalk at 2 to 3 oz. per tree will also be beneficial.

The chief disease to keep an eye open

for is bacterial canker which can also infect plums and other stone fruits. It is characterized by the sudden death of whole branches, usually accompanied by considerable exudation of resinous gum. An early sympton is the appearance of small round holes in the leaves, which also subsequently turn yellow. Cankering appears on the bark. There is no satisfactory cure and all affected branches should be removed immediately and the wounds painted with Stockholm tar or a bituminous wound dressing. Cherries are also subject to silver leaf disease (see page 89) and to brown rot which attacks the fruits causing a brownish disolouration of the skin followed by the emergence of greyish-brown tufts arranged in irregular circles. All infected fruit should be gathered and burned without delay. Prevention is always better than a cure and a regular spraying programme can be carried out to keep pests and diseases at bay [3]. Birds are a considerable nuisance while the young cherries are developing for they peck at the fruit. Fan-trained trees can be netted to protect them [4].

The pruning of a fan-shaped Morello cherry follows on similar lines to that for a fan-trained peach. Three or four main shoots form the skeleton of the fan with

the centre left free for training in the side shoots as they develop. Leave as many young branches in as possible and cut out some of the old wood each year for a Morello cherry, like the peach, bears its fruit on the young branches produced the previous year [5]. Tie in the new shoots as they develop during the spring [6].

Peaches The best way to grow peach trees out of doors are as fan-shaped specimens on a warm south-facing wall. Autumn or early winter is the best time to plant them as they come into flower early in the spring and require as much time as possible in the preceding season to get established. The ground should be well manured and then dressed with lime. A generous dressing of bonemeal should be applied also. If you are considering planting two or more trees against a wall they should be planted 10 to 12 ft. apart. In February or June of every year they should be heavily mulched with organic matter and watered freely in dry weather. An annual sprinkling of Nitro-chalk will also help good growth. The fruit will want thinning, starting when each is about the size of a walnut and this should be done gradually over several weeks, so that finally there is one left to every 9 in. of shoot growth [1].

The training and pruning of a fan-shaped peach tree is started by taking the two strongest side shoots and fanning them out one to each side. The strongest laterals of these are retained and tied in each year [2], gradually filling the centre as well as the sides. When new shoots start to grow up in spring, there will be far too many of them and it is

necessary to rub the unwanted ones away before they grow to any length [3]. On each fruit-bearing shoot remove all the new young laterals, a few at a time, until only two are left, one at the tip and one at or near the base. Where shoots appear with the fruit, reduce these to one and pinch this back to leave one leaf, which will help to feed the fruit.

In November, cut out the old fruiting growths [4] and tie in the basal shoot which grew during the summer to take its place. Prune back the leading shoots if more extension growth is required, otherwise prune right back to the replacement shoot.

If there are plenty of bees about when the peaches are in flower, no hand pollination is required. However, if the weather is windy and cold, I would advise pollinating with a rabbit's tail or, as you are unlikely to be able to get one, a piece of cotton wool attached to a stick. Lightly dust this along the opened flowers [5].

Peach leaf curl is a fungal disease which causes the leaves to curl as they become thickened and turn a red or purple colour [6]. It is usually worse in the spring and is aggravated by cold weather. Remove affected leaves and spray with Bordeaux mixture shortly

before the buds begin to swell the following year.

If the leaves take on a metallic silver appearance this is due to a condition known as silver leaf. If the wood is cut into on a branch carrying silver leaves it will be brown and discoloured. It cannot be controlled by spraying as the sap becomes infected. Sometimes the tree grows out of it but if it is spreading remove the affected branch, burn it and paint the wound with a sealing compound.

Varieties include Noblesse, Peregrine, Barrington and Hale's Early.

Raspberries I rate raspberries as the best soft fruit crop for the amateur to grow. They are excellent for deep freezing and if they are given a deep, rich, well-drained soil and an open sunny position they are easy to grow. Although they are traditionally thought of as summer fruiting, there are also autumn-fruiting varieties. Raspberries, unfortunately, are subject to virus infection and it is wise to buy stock which is certified free of this trouble, for which there is no cure.

Good varieties include Malling Promise, Lloyd George, Malling Jewel, and Norfolk Giant. Hailsham, Zeva and September are good autumn-fruiting raspberries.

Plant on a suitable day between November and March spacing the plants 2 ft. apart, in rows 5 ft. apart [1]. Firm planting is essential [2]. Raspberry canes are trained to wires which are strained between posts at either end of the row. Two rows of wires are sufficient, 2½ ft. and 5 ft. above the ground.

After planting cut back the canes to about 9 in. above soil level and do not let the canes bear any fruit the first year. Do not prune during the first year either and as the canes grow, tie them loosely to the wires with raffia or some

other soft material [3]. Mulch the plants each spring with well-rotted organic matter and feed with a dressing of a compound fertilizer at the rate recommended by the manufacturer each April – May [4]. Apply a further mulch in June. Raspberries are surface rooting so take care when hoeing to remove weeds. Water the plants freely if the weather is dry during the fruiting period.

Pruning of established summer-fruiting varieties consists of cutting out to ground level all the canes which have fruited immediately the crop has been gathered. At the same time cut out any weak, broken or diseased canes. Then reduce the number of new canes at each root or stool to the six strongest and tie these in to the wires, spacing them about 6 in. apart to give an even coverage of the area available [5]. These canes should be tipped in February or March. Autumn-fruiting varieties are pruned in February. All canes are cut to ground level and new canes are produced which will bear fruit that autumn.

Raspberries are increased by taking suckers with roots from the parent plant in autumn. Cut them off cleanly and make sure that the parent plant is free from virus [6].

Raspberry beetle is the chief pest of this fruit. The grub of the beetle feeds on the young fruits after hatching from eggs laid in the flowers. The fruits do not develop but they become brown and hard or ripen on one side only. Spray the canes with derris 10 days after petal fall and again a fortnight later and do this spraying in the evening when the bees have left the plants.

Raspberry cane spot is a disease of the canes which shows as purple or dark spots and patches. Growth is stunted, leaves may be shed and the buds may be killed. Spray with lime sulphur in March and again when the first flowers open.

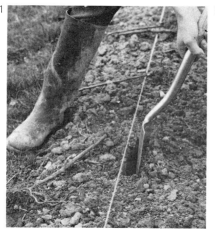

Laxtons No. 1 is a very popular variety of red currant. It gives high yields of good quality berries

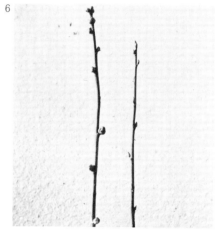

Blackcurrants Blackcurrants are grown as a bush with the main shoots arising from ground level instead of being borne on a short main stem, or leg as it is called, as is the case with red and white currants and gooseberries. Blackcurrants like a rich well-cultivated soil which is rather moist and a sunny or partially shaded position. Try not to plant in a windy position but if this is unavoidable protect them from the prevailing wind with hessian or sacking as a barrier otherwise they will suffer from what is known as run-off. Bees do not like wind and will not pollinate the blossom with the result that only one or two flowers near the top end of the strig, the name given to the bunch of fruit, are likely to set, the flowers getting progressively less well set the nearer they are to the free end of the strig.

Blackcurrants are sold as one or two-year-old bushes and should be planted between November and March, 6 ft. apart each way. They should be planted deeply so that the stems come through the soil rather than from above the soil [1]. It is important to get rid of of all perennial weeds before planting as blackcurrants fill the soil with a mass of fine roots making cultivation difficult once they have become established.

Immediately after planting cut the stems down to within 4 to 6 in. of soil level [2]. This is essential to ensure the production of plenty of good strong new shoots in the following season and it is on these that fruit will be produced a year later. There will be no fruit in the first season after planting and no pruning will be necessary during that year.

Each year, either in late winter or after fruiting in summer, the bushes should be mulched heavily with organic matter. A light potash dressing applied after fruiting in the summer will help to ripen the wood and encourage future fruit production [3]. Straw can be spread on the soil round the bushes to discourage weeds. It can be left down permanently and renewed as required.

Pruning is carried out after the fruit has been picked in the summer. Cut out all the stems which have just borne fruit to leave the new shoots which will flower and fruit the next year [4].

Blackcurrants are propagated by layering in June or July or by soft or hardwood cuttings. The softwood cuttings are taken in July and are made from the top 3 in. of the side growths. They are rooted in a shaded cold frame and lined out in rows outside in the autumn. Hardwood cuttings are taken from the current season's wood and are 10 in. long [5]. They are planted in a prepared trench in October so that only the top three or four buds remain above soil level. The other buds are not removed. The cuttings are spaced 9 in. apart and firmed well.

The main pest to keep an eye open for is the big bud mite which enters the dormant buds and causes them to become round and swollen [6]. Eventually the buds are killed. Many mites also carry a virus known as reversion which causes the leaves to become nettle-like and the bush produces very little fruit. There is no cure for the virus and affected bushes should be removed and burnt. The mite can be controlled by hand picking the affected buds or by spraying lime sulphur in the spring when the most forward leaves have reached 1 in. in diameter.

Varieties include Mendip Cross, Boskoup Giant, Wellington, Westwick Choice and Daniel's September.

Red and White Currants Red and white currants are both treated in a similar way to blackcurrants, except in respect to pruning for they are grown on a leg or short main stem. They should be planted [1] 4 to 6 ft. apart in rows the same distance apart and should be cut back after planting to leave about 6 in. of stem on the main side shoots, of which there should be four or five, any other side shoots being cut right out. The cuts should be made to buds pointing outwards and any pointing inwards should be rubbed off.

Red and white currants produce their fruits on the older stems, not on young stems like blackcurrants. A crop may be taken the first year after planting. The fruit buds are produced in little clusters which are quite prominent by the autumn so be careful not to cut any of these off when pruning. In the autumn shorten the main branches by about 6 in. and shorten side growths to leave one bud. A few well-placed side growths may be retained to form further main branches. Do not overcrowd the bush, however, and keep an open centre [2].

Red and white currants are propagated by hardwood cuttings in the same way as blackcurrants except that

only the top three or four buds are left on each cutting and the trenches in which they are planted are much shallower.

Good red currant varieties are Red Lake and Laxton's No. 1 ; white currants are well represented by White Dutch and White Versailles.

Gooseberries Gooseberries are also grown on a short leg. Two-year-old bushes are planted in the autumn or early winter, 5 to 6 ft. apart, in a well-drained soil which has been well manured beforehand. After planting cut all the shoots back, removing all but four or five strong shoots, and cutting away about three-quarters of each of these. In spring each year mulch heavily with organic matter and give a light dressing of potash [3].

Light pruning is carried out in the autumn. Ingrowing shoots are cut away entirely as are those which are crowded, crossing or diseased. The aim is to have an open-centred bush to let in light and air and to facilitate fruit picking [4]. Tip the leading shoots and only cut most of the side shoots back to three-quarters of their length. The rest can be cut back to one bud from the base. Some varieties have a drooping habit and this can be corrected by cutting back to an upward

pointing bud at the apex of the curve of the drooping shoots.

Gooseberries are increased by hardwood cuttings of one-year-old wood prepared in early October. They should be about 9 in. long and be inserted to two-thirds of their length in a light, sandy soil. As with red currants rub off all but the top four or five buds.

Gooseberries can be attacked by the larva of the gooseberry sawfly. This pest is green with black spots and feeds voraciously on the leaves and a colony can strip a bush very quickly. They appear in May, late June and mid-August and when spotted the bushes should be sprayed with derris [5]. The chief disease of gooseberries is american gooseberry mildew [6] which manifests itself on the leaves, fruits and stems first with a cobwebby appearance, later changing to a light, powdery condition. A neglected attack will turn brown and the stems become felted. Spray twice with lime-sulphur wash just before the bushes come into flower and again as soon as the fruit is set. Careless and Leveller are sulphur shy and dinocap should be used on these varieties instead. Several applications will be necessary, applied if possible in dry weather.

Two clematis varieties Ernest Markham and Mrs N. Thompson have been effectively planted
with the species *tangutica* to give this lovely show

Strawberries Strawberries like a warm, sunny site and a rather rich soil that has been deeply dug and enriched with well-rotted farmyard manure. They can be planted in late summer or early autumn or in March but spring-planted strawberries should not be allowed to fruit during the first year. The plant must be kept at surface level and the roots spread out well. The soil must be firm around the roots [1,2]. The best results are to be had from one-year-old plants and after three years they should be discarded. Strawberries are shallow-rooting plants and are weakened if they have to compete with weeds. The ground, therefore, must be weed free before planting.

Black polythene sheeting or clean straw [3] can be spread around the plants and under the leaves in May to keep the fruits clean. At this time, too, the bed can be covered with fish netting or plastic-covered wire netting to protect the developing fruits from the birds. If there are signs of mildew or other diseases and straw has been used burn this when all the fruit has been gathered. This will burn off the old foliage but new, disease-free leaves will soon appear. Remove all the runners which may develop unless they are wanted for propagating.

If the plants are covered with cloches in March they will produce ripe fruit in late May [4] in sheltered areas but make sure that the soil does not become dry when giving this protection. By using cloches and choosing one's varieties carefully the season can be spread over six or seven weeks in summer, with more fruit in the autumn if perpetual-fruiting varieties are grown.

The perpetual-fruiting varieties flower continuously from May onwards and produce good-sized and well-flavoured fruit in the autumn in abundance. The first blossoms, however, should be removed and only the later ones allowed to fruit. Perpetual-fruiting varieties can be planted 9 in. apart and be allowed to form a matted bed. They will throw runners which can be retained but the flowers from these runners should be taken off if strong plants are required the following year. Providing the plants with the protection of cloches in the autumn will result in larger fruits of better colour.

Strawberries are increased by plantlets formed on the runners. The plantlet on each runner nearest the plant should be chosen, the rest being removed. Between four and six should then be left on each parent plant. I sink small pots into the strawberry bed into which to root the runners. The rooted plantlets can then be transplanted with little or no check. The runners are pressed down with a bent piece of wire [5]. June and July are the best months for strawberry propagation and the plantlets should be well-rooted by the end of August. They can then be severed from the parent plants [6]. They should be left in position for about a week longer and then transferred to their permanent quarters.

Varieties include Cambridge Favourite, Royal Sovereign, Talisman and Redgauntlet. Sans Rival and St Claud are two good perpetual-fruiting varieties.

Vegetable Growing

Nowadays, I really do think that it is well worthwhile to set aside an area of the garden in which to grow vegetables. And, apart from any question of economics, there is great satisfaction to be gained from growing good produce of your own and there can be no doubt that home-grown vegetables are fresher and have more flavour. With careful management and planning even a relatively small area can be made to supply salads and some of the more high yielding crops such as runner beans, whilst an average allotment will produce enough vegetables for a family of four with the possible exception of main crop potatoes.

Growing vegetables is not difficult provided you are able to satisfy the three basic requirements of sun, sufficient water and good soil. Soil preparation should begin in the autumn with digging and the incorporation of compost or manure and I have dealt with all this on page 10. Many vegetables are heavy feeders and you should remember this when applying fertilizers. Beans, peas, leeks, lettuce, onions and celery are best on soil which has been recently manured. The brassicas should be grown on soil which has been dressed with fertilizer immediately before sowing and has been limed too, if necessary, and the root crops on soil which has had an application of general fertilizer but has not been recently manured.

Where space is limited it is particular important to master the techniques of successional sowing – sowing a little and often so that you are not left with a glut of any vegetable – and intercropping, which consists of sowing quick-maturing crops such as lettuce and radish between crops which occupy the ground for longer periods. In order to make maximum use of the area I feel that cloches are essential items of equipment. These will provide protection for newly planted seedlings or for crops which mature late in the year and so enable you to use the ground over a longer period. And if you are short of space why not plan to grow some vegetables in pots or tubs, runner beans, french beans, early potatoes and tomatoes are all good for growing in this way.

When it comes to choosing varieties there is much room for experimenting as both yields and flavours vary with soils and it is always wise to enquire of local gardeners which kinds do best in your area.

Unfortunately vegetables are subject to a number of pests and diseases and you should keep a strict watch for any occurrences.

Brassicas This is a group name for all the cabbages, broccoli, cauliflower, brussels sprouts, savoy and kale. All have much the same cultivation requirements and need quite a lot of space and rich, well-drained soil. The last is essential if you are to grow crops with good solid hearts and curds.

Prepare the seed bed by treading the soil to make it really firm [1], then apply a dressing of general fertilizer at 2 oz. to the sq. yd. Rake the soil to obtain a fine even surface and sow the seeds thinly in shallow drills [2] which may be taken out with a corner of the hoe or a piece of pointed stick. Shuffle the soil back into the drills with the feet. A final rake over will leave the seed bed tidy and remove footmarks. Always label the rows as you go. Sowing times for these vegetables will be found on page 117.

Dust along the rows of seedlings occasionally with 4 per cent. calomel dust to control cabbage root fly and club root. Once the seedlings have germinated they should be pulled gently and transplanted. Here [3], I am pulling brussels sprouts. These small seedlings are then planted out at the distances given in the table on page 117 and for this job I like to mark the row with a line and use a dibber [4] to make the hole. The plant is set in place down to the level of the lower leaves and is firmed by pushing the dibber in about 1 in. away and levering the soil towards the plant [5].

For an early start, the seeds can be sown in a garden frame and given protection until they have germinated. Harden them off by increasing ventilation gradually until the frame lights have been removed and, once a few leaves have been formed, lift the plants for replanting in the open ground [6]. I use a trowel to do this to ensure that a good ball of soil is retained around the roots. The plants are then set out in the garden [7] and I would point out here that with all the brassicas it is important to plant firmly in well-dug and reasonably rich soil. Before transplanting dip the roots in a paste of 4 per cent. calomel dust and water to prevent serious trouble from club root disease. Young brassicas suffer badly if inadequately watered, so do give plenty of water after planting and in light or rather dry soil this is more effective if the plants are set in a shallow trench when they are planted [8].

Routine cultivation for the brassicas includes frequent hoeing to remove competition from weeds and to break down the surface of the soil to form a fine mulch which helps to conserve moisture in the lower layers. I also feed my plants with small topdressings of a general fertilizer. This is sprinkled around the plants and hoed in but do take care to stir the soil gently so as not to destroy any roots which may be near the surface [1]. When to feed varies with the crops, broccoli, brussels sprouts, summer, autumn and winter varieties of cabbage are all fed in the summer, while spring cabbage and cauliflowers should not be fed until danger of prolonged frost is over, say in March and April. Winter greens benefit from a feed in early autumn.

As brassicas are subject to a number of pests and diseases you should keep a strict watch for any such appearances. In fact, I give a routine dusting of gamma BHC occasionally as a preventive measure against depredations of cabbage root fly and flea beetle [2].

Many of the brassicas are heavy plants and those which are to stand through the winter should be given some additional support to help them withstand heavy winds. Spring cabbage, which is planted out in September and October, can be earthed up to provide better anchorage [3] but brussels sprouts are better if individually staked [4]. After strong winds and frosts I think it is worth going over the vegetable plot and refirming any plants which have been loosened.

Both cauliflower and heading broccoli produce close heads of flowers known as curds and there is no real difference between them. However, the term cauliflower is used for the more tender summer varieties and the term broccoli for the hardier autumn and spring kinds. But whichever kind is grown it is important to turn some of the leaves inwards [5] to protect the curds from the weather and keep them white. Cut the curds when they are well grown [6]. The other sort of broccoli is the sprouting kind [7] which produces a succession of flowering shoots for cutting as required.

Picking of brussels sprouts can usually begin in late November, starting at the bottom of the stem and taking the largest 'buttons' first [8]. The yellowing leaves can be removed at any time and when all the sprouts have been picked, not before, do not forget that the tops of the plants are useful as a winter vegetable.

Legumes This is another conveniently collective name for the group of vegetables which includes the various types of beans – broad, french and runner – and also the peas. They need a rich, well-dug and well-manured soil and close attention to watering if they are to be grown successfully.

BROAD BEANS These can be sown in deep boxes in the greenhouse in February or in the open ground in March. In mild areas longpod varieties can be sown out of doors in November. If the seeds are sown in boxes [1] they should be hardened off in a frame [2] for planting out of doors in April. But outside I prefer to sow the beans in wide drills which have been taken out with a spade. Make the drills 2 in. deep and place the beans in a double row with 4 to 6 in. between the beans [3] and 3 ft. between the double rows. After sowing and labelling the rows draw the soil over the beans with a rake [4].

I keep the hoe going between the rows throughout the season and draw a little soil up round them in severe weather. It is important to stake against wind damage using stout posts connected by strings. When the plants have set their flowers pinch out the growing tips [5] to encourage the beans to develop and to lessen the chances of attack by blackfly. Unfortunately the beans are very susceptible to attack by these insects and it will be necessary to spray at intervals using an insecticide containing menazon [6]. It is especially important when growing food crops to follow the manufacturer's instructions for the application of insecticides, particularly those relating to the time which must be allowed to elapse between spraying and harvesting.

Pick the beans when they are young and about 8 to 10 in. long [7].

FRENCH BEANS Sow in late April or early May in drills 1 in. deep and 2 ft. apart and space the seeds 6 in. apart in the drills. To produce early crops, I like to make a sowing in pots in a greenhouse in January or February. Sow 5 or 6 seeds in a 3½-in. pot in John Innes No. 1 compost and repot into 7-in. pots of John Innes No. 3 compost.

Climbing french beans are grown in the same way except that the rows should be spaced at least 3 ft. apart and some form of support provided.

It is important to gather the beans regularly as soon as they reach a usable size [8].

RUNNER BEANS These require a rich, well-manured soil. They are rather tender and it is not really safe to sow out of doors before the end of April and mid-May is the more generally suitable time. For a later crop another sowing can be made in June. The seeds are sown singly about 2 in. deep and 9 to 12 in. apart in a double row [1]. Allow 12 in. between the two rows of seeds and 5 ft. between successive pairs of rows. Each plant must be given some form of support and here I have used long poles. These in turn are lashed to a cross bar near the top to provide extra stability. There are, of course, other ways of training beans. They can be grown up vertical stakes, up strings secured to a central pole in maypole fashion, up wires or up plastic netting which is sold specifically for this purpose.

For an early crop I sow runner beans under glass towards the end of April. Sow the seeds individually in small pots of John Innes No. 1 compost and harden the plants off for planting out in late May or early June. I prepare the bed by putting in stakes and then set one plant beside each stake [2]. Water well after planting and remember that a good supply of water must be given throughout the growing season if you

are to achieve a good crop. Hoeing between the rows will keep down weeds and conserve soil moisture [3].

To ensure a good set of beans I always spray my plants with clear water when they are in flower. A routine spray with an insecticide containing menazon or dimethoate will help to control blackfly. Finally, as the beans will soon become tough and stringy if left on the plants, pick frequently.

PEAS To get an early start with peas I sow them in pots in the greenhouse early in February, 4 to 5 seeds in each $3\frac{1}{2}$-in. pot [4]. This is a worthwhile practice in northern or other cold districts.

There are two main kinds of peas: wrinkled-seeded and round-seeded, and it is varieties of the former which should be used for sowing under glass. It is important to grow the plants without much heat to ensure that they grow sturdily. Planting out can be done in late March in a warm sheltered border after the plants have been hardened off. Cloches are useful to provide added protection in the early part of the year [5].

Outdoor sowing can start in late February in sheltered areas using round-seeded varieties. Sow in wide,

shallow trenches in triple rows [6], spacing the seeds 3 to 4 in. apart each way and covering them with 2 in. of soil. Support should be given from an early stage.

Further sowings of the wrinkled-seeded varieties can be made at fortnightly intervals until early June to give a succession of cropping.

Water well, keep the surrounding soil well hoed and spray occasionally with BHC or dimethoate against attacks of pea thrips. These small insects cause distortion and a silvering of the pods. Spraying with BHC or dimethoate 10 days after flowering begins will also protect against pea maggots.

Picking should be done a little at a time as the pods fill up and you will find that the lower pods fill first.

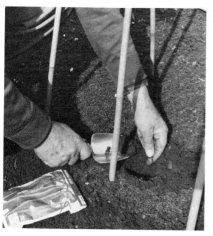

Root crops In the main these are easy crops to grow. All require a good deeply worked soil which has not been freshly manured but has been dressed with a general fertilizer at 2 to 4 oz. to the sq. yd. before sowing.

PARSNIP The seeds are sown from March to early April and I sow 2 or 3 seeds together [1] at 9-in. intervals in drills 1 in. deep and 18 in. apart. These are later singled leaving the strongest plant at each position [2]. In the autumn the roots should be lifted carefully. Badly forked roots [3] are caused by growing in soil which is very stony or has been freshly manured. The roots can be stored in a shed or cellar or they can be left in the ground and dug up as required, but this may be difficult if the ground freezes.

CARROT Sowing of the early varieties can begin out of doors in March but main crop carrots should not be sown before mid-April. Sowings of small successional batches can continue until mid-July.

Sow the seeds thinly in shallow drills 8 to 12 in. apart depending on variety; the long-rooted and intermediate types requiring the bigger distance, shorthorn and stump-rooted the smaller. The resulting seedlings are thinned to 4 to 8 in. apart [4].

Apart from hoeing the most important cultural routine is to dust the soil with naphthalene every 10 days from thinning time until the end of June to eradicate carrot fly.

The roots are lifted when they are large enough to use [5] and before they split. Main crop varieties lifted in October can be stored in deep boxes of fairly dry sand. I cut the top growth from the carrots and then put them in boxes in layers [6], covering each layer with sand or ashes.

BEETROOT The seeds are sown in clusters 6 to 8 in. apart in drills 1 in. deep and 15 in. apart from April to July. Thin the seedlings to leave the strongest plant in each position. Keep well hoed and for use in summer salads lift the roots as required [7]. Main crop varieties can be lifted in October and stored in the same way as carrots.

TURNIPS AND SWEDES These two vegetables are very similar in appearance except that the swede has a more pronounced neck [8]. Sow the seeds successively from March to August in shallow drills 12 to 15 in. apart and thin the seedlings to 6 to 8 in. apart. Feed occasionally with a general fertilizer. They can be stored in a frostproof shed.

Potatoes I do not think it is worth growing a main crop of potatoes if space is limited as they take up so much room for such a long time. However, I do like to grow a few rows of early potatoes and also some in pots for even earlier cropping.

In January when the seed potatoes arrive I start them forming sprouts by standing them eye upwards in boxes. I do recommend that you buy seed potatoes which are certified as being free of virus. The seed tubers are kept in cool but frostproof conditions until they produce short, sturdy sprouts. Before planting, I rub off some of these sprouts to leave two or three [1].

Planting of the earlies can start in mid-March. After forking the plot I take out a 5-in. V-shaped trench [2].

The tubers are planted 15 to 18 in. [3] apart in rows 2½ to 3 ft. apart and are covered with 2 to 3 in. of soil initially [4]. The process of earthing up is a gradual one which should begin when the shoots appear through the soil and it simply involves drawing soil up over the shoots. The earthing up is continued until the potatoes are growing in ridges. The tubers will be ready for lifting in June or July [5].

If you have the space to grow a main crop, then you should proceed as outlined above but set the tubers out in April. Subsequent cultivation is also the same and, in addition, from June onwards I spray with a copper fungicide against potato blight. This can be very troublesome in a wet season, and the foliage will soon become blackened if spraying is not carried out.

Lifting of main crop varieties can begin in September or October and this should be done carefully, using a fork and working well away from the plants to avoid damage to the tubers. Main crop tubers can be stored in sacks in a frost-free shed.

I always think that some pots of an early potato such as the variety Home Guard are an essential to give tubers for eating in April and May. Sprout the tubers in the same way as previously described and then plant them, 3 to an 8 or 9-in. pot on John Innes No. 3 compost and peat in equal parts. Half fill the pots and put the potatoes 1½ to 2 in. deep, then as they grow topdress with the same compost to bring the level to within an inch of the top [6, 7, 8].

Onions These require a crumbly, well-worked soil. The seeds can be sown in a greenhouse in late December or January and the seedlings pricked out and hardened off for planting outside in late April.

I like to sow the seeds out of doors either early in March where the plants are to mature or in early autumn in a sheltered nursery bed from which they can be transplanted in the following spring. In both cases the soil should be well firmed and the seeds sown in shallow drills spaced 12 in. apart. When large enough, the spring sown onions are thinned [1] and the thinnings used in salads. The final spacing in the rows should leave the bulbs 6 in. apart.

If you have had difficulty in raising plants from seed then a good alternative is to plant onion sets. Do this in March or April and space the sets 6 in. apart in rows 12 in. apart.

I hoe between the rows from time to time to keep the weeds down [2] and dust with lindane or 4 per cent. calomel dust against onion fly. Water well in dry weather and in June or July a little general fertilizer sprinkled along the rows at about 10-day intervals will encourage sturdy growth [3].

In late August the tops are bent over to assist ripening [4]. In early September when the bulbs have developed fully, lift them and lay them out to dry in the sun. With our uncertain climate, I space mine in a garden frame [5] and cover them with a light to give protection from rain. Then clean them and store by plaiting the dry leaves together in ropes and hanging them up in a dry shed [6]. Alternatively, they may be hung up in net bags.

Shallots Looking like small onions, shallots can either be used as a substitute for onions or for pickling. They require a sunny position, well-drained deeply-dug soil which should not be too firm as this encourages the bulbs to work their way up on to the surface.

Shallots are grown from small bulbs which are planted 6 to 9 in. apart in rows 12 in. apart in February or early March [7]. Alternatively, seeds can be sown in drills 8 in. apart in March. Hoe frequently and in June remove a little soil from around the bulbs to assist ripening. The tops are turned down [8] and the shallots lifted, dried and stored as for onions.

Leeks This vegetable requires a deep, rich, well-manured soil. The seeds can either be sown in a greenhouse in January or February and hardened off for planting outside in May or sown in a seed bed out of doors in March [1] and transplanted to their cropping position in June. When planting leeks I make holes 6 to 8 in. deep and 9 in. apart with a dibber and drop one leek plant into each hole [2]. There is no need to replace the soil, all that is required to settle them in is to fill each hole with water [3]. Hoe frequently in summer, water freely and feed every 10 days or so with weak liquid manure or with a general fertilizer. As the plants develop I draw soil up around each one to get an extra length of blanched stem [4].

Leeks can be lifted as needed from late autumn onwards, although before bad weather sets in I think it is a good idea to lift a few extra and heel them in [5,6] in a sheltered part of the garden where they can easily be got at in frosty or snowy weather.

Spinach There are two kinds of spinach, the summer or round-seeded kind and the winter or prickly-seeded kind and by growing both sorts it is possible to have a supply throughout the year.

As spinach is a fast-growing crop it is essential to have a well-dug and well-manured soil, preferably with a good lime content. Seeds of summer spinach can be sown in small batches from mid-March to mid-July, those of winter spinach in mid-August or even later in sheltered areas. I sow the seeds in 1-in. deep drills set 1 ft. apart, and thin gradually to 9 in. (4 in. is sufficient for the winter kind).

Water liberally in dry weather, spinach does not take kindly to hot, dry conditions and will run up to seed if you are not careful. Gather the leaves as soon as they are of a usable size [7]. In cooler areas, it is a good idea to protect winter spinach with cloches during very cold periods.

Spinach beet This is a form of beetroot grown for its leaves [8] which are used like spinach. It is very hardy and can withstand hot conditions better than spinach.

To maintain a regular supply, sow the seeds in two batches, one in early April and the other at the beginning of August. Sow in 1-in. deep drills set 18 in. apart and thin the seedlings to 9 in. apart. Once they reach a usable size pick the leaves continuously, pulling them from the outside of the plants.

Lettuce These like a well-manured soil and I cannot stress too much the importance of sowing little and often so that you are not left with a glut of plants all ready for harvesting at the same time.

For the earliest crops a sowing can be made in pots or boxes in February. Prick out the seedlings [1], taking care to handle them by the leaves only, and harden them off for planting out of doors in late March or early April. Set the plants at intervals of 9in. and if the soil is at all dry water the planting area well before putting the young plants in [2]. Lettuce are especially vulnerable to dry conditions and should always be kept well watered.

Outdoor sowings can be made at fortnightly intervals from early March until mid-August. I sow the seeds thinly in drills 12in. apart [3] and then shuffle the soil back with my feet; a final raking will remove footmarks [4]. The seedlings must be thinned out as soon as they are large enough to handle [5], leaving the plants between 9 and 12in. apart. The thinnings need not be wasted, I transplant them to an area further along the row where they will give a slightly later crop.

If the earliest sowings are covered with cloches [6] cropping dates can be advanced to produce a supply of lettuce when they are scarce and expensive.

Keep the plants well hoed throughout the season.

Selected varieties are also available for sowing in late August or early September in the open ground in a sheltered place. They will reach maturity in the early spring. Plant the seedlings 9in. apart in rows 12in. apart in early October and I put slug pellets down the rows in late autumn and early spring. Once again if some of the plants can be covered with cloches cutting can be advanced by a couple of weeks.

There are still other varieties for sowing in frames [7] or greenhouses [8] in the autumn to provide lettuce for eating in winter and spring.

All the winter lettuces benefit from a dressing of a general fertilizer in February or March. This can be sprinkled round the plants and hoed gently into the soil but it must be kept off the leaves. Go over winter lettuce plants occasionally and remove decaying leaves to prevent spread of disease, and keep a close watch for greenfly which often affects lettuce in the early spring.

Chicory This is a succulent winter salad crop which is not grown nearly often enough in my opinion. Seeds are sown thinly in early June in $\frac{1}{2}$-in. deep drills set 15 in. apart and the seedlings are thinned to 1 ft. apart. Keep the rows hoed and remove any flowering shoots which may appear. In November dig up the roots carefully [1] and cut off the leaves about 1 in. above the crowns. Trim the roots back to about 8 in. in length and store them in sand in a cool shed until they are needed for forcing. If you force a few at a time from late November onwards you will have a succession of the tightly packed hearts of leaves or 'chicons' throughout the winter.

To force, take the roots out of the sand as required and pack them in large pots with some old potting soil, three roots to each 7-in. pot is sufficient [2]. Another flower pot is inverted over the one containing the roots and the drainage hole is covered to exclude all light [3]. Forcing is best carried out in a warm greenhouse, shed or cellar in a temperature of at least 10°C. (50°F.). After a few weeks the thick shoots are blanched [4] and can be cut off at ground level. Discard the roots after forcing.

Endive This looks rather like a curly leaved lettuce and it is blanched for use in summer or winter salads. The seeds are sown from April onwards in $\frac{1}{2}$-in. deep drills and the seedlings are thinned to 9 in. apart. Little attention is needed except for hoeing between the rows and as this crop should be grown quickly I give a couple of topdressings of nitrate of soda or Nitro-chalk at 1 oz. to 12 ft. of row.

When the plants are well grown they can be blanched by inverting a flower pot over them [5]. Make sure all light is excluded by putting a tile or piece of wood over the drainage hole. Leave them until the leaves are creamy white, taking about six weeks.

Radish Radishes are a very fast-growing crop, particularly useful as a catch crop for sowing between slow-growing vegetables such as celery. Seeds should be sown frequently in small batches from March to mid-August. Sow in $\frac{1}{2}$-in. deep drills set about 6 in. apart. Little after-care is necessary, as with all the vegetables I keep the rows well hoed and give plenty of water in dry weather. Some protection from birds may be required [6]. To be tasted at their best radishes must be grown quickly.

Tomatoes This popular crop can be grown either in a greenhouse or in a sheltered sunny position out of doors. There are a large number of varieties for both methods of culture and in addition there are bush tomatoes, so called because they are allowed to grow without the removal of side shoots and consequently produce low freely branched plants which need little or no support. Most tomatoes, however, are restricted to a single stem and do require some method of support.

GREENHOUSE CULTIVATION For growing under glass, I sow the seeds very thinly in mid-March [1] and germinate them in a temperature of around 16 to 18°C. (60 to 65°F.). Prick the seedlings out and once they are large enough to handle, pot them off singly into 3½-in. pots of John Innes No. 1 compost [2]. When they reach a height of 4 in. repot into 5-in. pots and later on pot again into 9-in. pots of John Innes No. 3 compost or a good loamy soil. Alternatively, plant in beds of good soil, spacing the plants 1½ ft. apart and staking each one [3]. Tomatoes must be given good support either from canes or soft string secured to the rafters or to a wire strained beneath the rafters. Grow the plants

throughout in a light position and do not let the temperature fall below 13°C. (55°F.).

As the plants grow, remove the side shoots which form in the axils of the leaves [4], this will restrict growth to one main stem. Tie [5] or train the plants in [6] to their supports as they grow. From May onwards I spray the flowers with water [7] at mid-day as this helps them to set fruit. Pinch out the growing tips when they reach the glass [8] and water the plants moderately at first but increasing the quantity as they grow. Once the first fruits have set, feed every week with a proprietary tomato fertilizer.

RING CULTURE This is another popular way of growing tomatoes both under glass and out of doors. It has the advantage of using less soil combined with a lower risk of infections entering the plants from the soil. This method encourages the formation of two different root systems: fine feeding roots in the pots of soil and a coarser root system for the uptake of water in the aggregate bed. Grow the plants as previously described until they have formed good root systems in their 3½-in. pots. Each plant is then planted in a special bottomless ring in John Innes No. 3

compost [9,10]. The rings, which are usually made of bituminized paper, are stood on a 6-in. deep bed of gravel, coarse sand or ash. Initially the soil in the rings is watered [11] but after the first few weeks when the roots have had sufficient time to penetrate into the aggregate bed water is applied freely to the gravel or ashes only [12]. Feeding is done into the soil in the bottomless pots when the first fruits begin to form and I like to give the plants a weekly liquid feed of a proprietary tomato fertilizer. The plants should be staked and grown on as previously described.

OUTDOOR CULTIVATION Sow the seeds in twos in 3½-in. pots of John Innes seed compost in a greenhouse in late March or early April and germinate in a temperature of 16°C. (60°F.). Thin the seedlings to leave the strongest in each pot. In May move the young plants to a frame and harden them off for planting out of doors in early June.

Make sure that the soil has been well dug and contains plenty of well-rotted compost or manure and set the plants out 1½ ft. apart in rows 2½ ft. apart [13]. Choose a sunny sheltered and, if possible, south-facing position. Plant firmly and support the stems against

canes or stakes [14], tying the stems in as the plants grow. An important routine job is the removal of the side shoots as they appear, in order to keep the plants to a single stem though this is unnecessary if you are growing the bush varieties as these are allowed to grow naturally into low, branched bushes which do not need staking. All other aspects of cultivation of the bush varieties are the same as for single-stemmed kinds.

It is essential to water well in warm weather and I find that a good way of doing this is to sink a 5-in. pot about 6 in. away from each plant at the time of planting. The pot can then be filled with water as often as required and the water will soak into the soil to reach the plants at root level.

As it is not possible to ripen more than four trusses of fruit in the open I pinch out the main growing points as soon as the fourth truss has been set. Once two trusses have formed I start to feed the plants weekly with a tomato fertilizer applied in a ring round the stem and well watered in.

Tomatoes are members of the potato family and they are liable to be infected with potato blight, which causes the leaves to go black, and in order to

prevent this I give a routine spray in early July with a copper fungicide.

To help the lower trusses to ripen it may be necessary to remove some of the foliage and, from the end of September when there is danger of frost at night, it is advisable to pick the fruits as they begin to show colour and to ripen them off in a warm dark place such as an airing cupboard. To speed up ripening at this time of year, I often untie the plants from their stakes, lay them on straw on the ground and cover them with cloches.

Tomatoes can be grown out of doors using the ring culture method. The procedure has already been described and the only variation is to remember to stop the plants once the fourth truss has been set.

Cucumber There are two types of cucumber: the frame kind for growing in greenhouses and frames and the ridge kind for growing out of doors.

FRAME CUCUMBERS Seeds of varieties of the frame cucumber are sown in twos in small pots in a temperature of about 18°C. (65°F.) at intervals from March until late April. After germination thin to leave one seedling in each pot. The fruiting beds can be prepared either on the floor of a greenhouse or on the staging. In either case the growing medium should be John Innes No. 3 compost or a mixture of soil, leafmould and well-rotted manure. A ridge of compost about 15 in. wide and 7 in. deep is sufficient for the young plants, which should be set out at intervals of 3 to 5 ft. Whenever roots appear on the surface [1] they should be covered with a further layer of compost. The plants will require support and this can be provided by canes, alternatively the shoots may be tied to wires strained horizontally along the house.

It is also possible to grow cucumbers in large pots [2]. Once again John Innes No. 3 compost can be used as the growing medium and some room should be left in the pots for a topdressing of the same compost as the plants grow.

Main growths should be allowed to run until they reach the apex of the roof and then the tops can be pinched out. Side growths are trained horizontally and are stopped at the second leaf joint [3]. Cucumbers usually produce both male and female flowers and if allowed to pollinate each other the resulting fruits will have a bitter taste. It is necessary to remove the male flowers [4] before pollination occurs. Distinguishing between the sexes is easy as the male flower has a straight slender stem while the female flower shows the tiny immature fruit immediately behind the petals. With the new all-female varieties this will be unnecessary.

Spray the plants daily with clear water and shade from strong sunshine. Weak liquid feeds can be given as soon as the first fruits start to grow.

Cucumbers can be planted in heated frames in April and in unheated frames at the end of May or early in June. For this purpose, seed should be sown in March. Plant on mounds of good compost and stop the plants by pinching out the growing tip when they have produced about six leaves. Stopping the plants will make them produce laterals, four of which I allow to develop. These are trained to the four

corners of the frame. Maintain a warm, moist atmosphere and shade the glass to prevent the sun from scorching the plants. Once again it is necessary to remove the male flowers. Water liberally, spray [5], feed and topdress the plants as described previously.

As the fruits develop I place a piece of glass or block of wood under each to raise it off the soil.

RIDGE CUCUMBERS These are much hardier than the other kind and can be grown out of doors in a sheltered sunny position [6]. Sow the seeds in mid-April in twos in 3½-in. pots and thin to leave one seedling in each pot. Harden off and plant out 3 to 4 ft. apart in late May on ridges of good soil and well-rotted compost. Seeds can be sown outside in mid-May. Pinch out the tip when six leaves have formed and train in the side shoots. Water freely and feed with liquid manure from the time the first fruits form. With ridge cucumbers it is important that the female flowers are pollinated so do not remove the male ones.

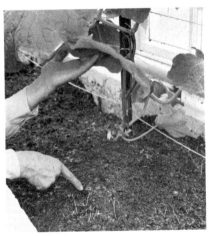

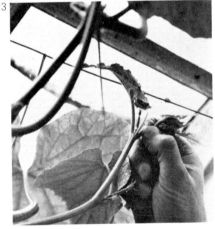

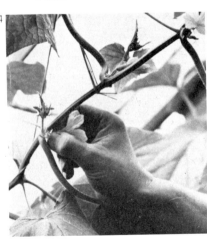

Marrows These require a rich loamy soil mixed with rotted manure or compost and I find that it is best to take out a 2-ft. deep hole [1] or a trench 2 ft. wide and 2 ft. deep and fill this with the soil and compost mixture [2].

Sow the seeds in April in a greenhouse, two to each 3½-in. pot, and germinate in a temperature of 18°C. (65°F.). Thin to leave the best seedling in each pot [3]. Out of doors sowing should not be attempted before mid-May and then the seeds should be covered with cloches or jam jars until they have germinated.

Plant out in the prepared position in early June [4], setting the bush varieties 3 ft. apart and the trailing ones 4 ft. apart. I like to cover the young plants with cloches for the first week after planting. When the runners of the trailing varieties have reached a length of about 3 ft. pinch out the ends as this will help the production of side shoots which usually carry the female flowers. But if too many side shoots are produced then they should be thinned out. Bush marrows, such as the courgette, require no pinching or thinning.

I find it is unwise to rely on insect pollination of the female flowers (those with embryo marrows behind the flower) and it is much safer to carry out the pollination yourself by picking the male flowers, removing most of the petals, and dusting the pollen into the centre of the female ones [5].

Keep the plants well supplied with water and feed with liquid manure as soon as the first marrows start to swell [6]. As the marrows develop put a sheet of glass under them to keep them off the soil. In the autumn cut any remaining marrows and store them in a frostproof shed, hanging them up in nets or string bags so that the air can circulate around them.

There are several kinds of marrow and many varieties of each. The bush type is the best for average sized gardens and this includes the courgette or zucchini, the very popular smaller type which can be successfully grown in tubs. The trailing type produce the familiar long, striped marrows.

As novelties there are the custard marrows with pumpkin-shaped fruits and the vegetable spaghetti, an oval marrow which gets its name from the fact that the inside looks like spaghetti.

Celery There are three types of celery – the white and pink or red, which both require blanching and the self-blanching which does not. This is a crop which needs well-dug and well-manured soil and requires a lot of water throughout the season.

Because the seeds are small and germinate slowly it is best to raise the young plants in a greenhouse, sowing the seeds any time from late February to early March. Harden the young plants off for planting outside in May or early June. Before planting I sprinkle a dressing of general fertilizer along the trench at 1½ oz. to the yard run and fork this in. Set the plants about a foot apart in the trenches which should be 6 in. deep, 18 in. to 2 ft. wide and 3 ft. apart. Soak well with water.

The self-blanching type does not need to be planted in a trench as it does not require any earthing up. With this kind of celery set the plants out in blocks 9 in. apart in each direction [1].

Celery should be fed regularly with weak liquid manure or general fertilizer [2,3] once the plants are well established.

In early August I start to blanch the celery (white, pink or red kinds) by earthing up the stems. First, remove all side growths [4] then wrap newspaper around the stems and tie with raffia [5] but make sure you allow room for the hearts to develop. Draw the soil up around the plants [6]. Blanching takes between six and eight weeks and as the plants grow I draw up more soil around them until only the top tuft of leaves is left exposed. In autumn or winter you may find it necessary to protect the exposed tops with straw or bracken.

Celeriac This is closely related to celery but it is the bulbous growth between the roots and leaf stems which is the useful part [7] and this can be cooked whole or shredded for use in salads. Like celery this vegetable requires a well-dug and manured soil.

I sow the seeds in a greenhouse in March or April and harden the seedlings off for planting outside in May where they should be set 1 ft. apart in rows 1½ ft. apart. No earthing up is needed [8], frequent hoeing and liberal watering are the only subsequent attentions required. In late summer, the roots can be lifted and stored in sand in an airy shed.

Celery is a versatile and delicious vegetable but it does demand a heavily manured soil and a lot of water throughout the season

Rhubarb To grow well, rhubarb requires well-drained soil and a sunny position. The divisions or crowns should be planted in February or March and set out so that they are 2 in. below the surface of the soil and 3 ft. apart each way. During the first year I make a point of not gathering any of the stalks as this gives the crowns time to build up in size. Topdress the plants with manure or compost each February and with general fertilizer when pulling is finished. Remove all the flower stalks as soon as these appear [1] and keep the plants well watered.

Cropping can begin in the second year and the young stalks should be pulled away cleanly from the crowns – a few at a time from each plant. Without forcing, the rhubarb will be ready for pulling in mid-April but earlier sticks can be obtained by covering the crowns with upturned buckets or boxes in January or February, and further protection and warmth is given by putting sacking [2] or a covering of leaves and compost over the bucket.

It is possible to obtain even earlier supplies by lifting some of the strong roots from November onwards and packing them with soil in deep boxes. These boxes should be put in a shed or cellar or under the greenhouse staging and you must make sure most of the light is excluded. Keep the plants moist and warm and you will have sticks for pulling in three or four weeks [3]. It is a good idea to expose the roots to frost for a few days before bringing them inside. Discard roots after forcing.

Sweet corn This really grows quite well in this country if you can give it well-manured soil and a sunny position. The seeds should be sown under glass in late April or early May and the seedlings hardened off for planting outside in late May. Space the plants 15 in. apart in rows 3 ft. apart and it is important to make short rows to produce blocks [4] of plants as this will assist pollination which is by wind. The male flowers are carried at the top of the plant and the female flowers which will produce the cobs lower down [5].

Water well in dry weather, hoe frequently and feed the plants with a general fertilizer in June. To taste the corn at its best the cobs must be harvested while young [6] and once the silk at the ends of the cobs goes brown you should test for readiness by puncturing one of the seeds with a knife point or fingernail. If a milky juice exudes then pick at once.

Herbs The majority of the herbs are not difficult to grow and since they need only occupy a small area of ground, in fact many will grow very satisfactorily in pots and window boxes, I think that they are a must for the garden. Ideally they should be placed as near to the kitchen door as possible and this is where the pot-grown ones can be especially useful. Most of the herbs have much the same cultivation requirements of a light well-draining soil and a sunny sheltered position. For growing in pots I use John Innes No. 1 compost. When cutting leaves for use, be selective and take care not to strip the plants.

When it comes to propagation, the herbs fall roughly into two groups: the annual ones which are increased by seed sown outside in May or under glass in March, and the shrubby perennial kinds, such as sage and thyme, which can be increased by half-ripe cuttings taken in August or September or heel cuttings taken in April or May. The shrubby perennials can also be increased by division of the root clumps in autumn or spring.

Many of the herbs can be dried and stored for future use. Pick the leaves in summer, usually when the flowers are beginning to open, and lay them in boxes or trays covered with muslin. Keep the boxes in a warm airy place and turn the leaves frequently. When the leaves become brittle pack them in air-tight containers.

My first choice of herbs for growing is parsley, sage, thyme, mint and chives. Parsley [1] is usually grown as an annual and to maintain a year-round supply I make three sowings, one in early March, the second in late May and the third in August. Grow in rich well-dug soil.

Sage [2] and thyme [3] can be grown from cuttings and should be cut back after flowering and divided every 3 or 4 years in late February. Both will only flourish in hot dry positions and a light sandy soil.

Mint presents a particular problem because it is so invasive that it will take over the garden if not checked. It is a perennial which spreads by runners and I always plant the runners in a bucket [4] or old tin bath which has been sunk in the soil, this effectively checks the spread of the plant. Mint will grow in either full sun or partial shade and prefers a moisture-retentive soil.

Chives [5] are perennials which grow well in ordinary soil or in pots and window boxes. The top growth dies down in winter and new leaves are produced from early May. Divide the plants in spring if necessary. Chives can be started from seeds sown in March. Water well in dry weather and give a topdressing of compost in early spring.

Fennel is also worth a mention as it has two uses, the leaves for flavouring and the swollen stem bases as a vegetable [6]. It is a perennial, which grows to a height of 6 ft. and needs a position at the back of the bed. Increase by division in spring or from seeds sown in late March.

Clever plant associations can bring much pleasure. Here *Euphorbia myrsinites* provides a
perfect foil to the primroses

Vegetable	Main sowing period	Depth of sowing	Transplant	Distance between rows	Distance between plants	Main harvesting period
Broccoli	April to May	$\frac{1}{2}$ in.	May to June	3 ft.	3 ft.	Sept. to June
Brussels sprouts	March	$\frac{1}{2}$ in.	April to May	3 ft.	3 ft.	Sept. to Feb.
Cabbage, summer	March	$\frac{1}{2}$ in.	April to May	2 ft.	$1\frac{1}{2}$ ft.	July to June
Cabbage, autumn & winter	March to May	$\frac{1}{2}$ in.	May to June	2 ft.	$1\frac{1}{2}$ ft.	July to June
Cabbage, spring	July to Aug.	$\frac{1}{2}$ in.	Sept. to Oct.	$1\frac{1}{2}$ ft.	1 ft.	July to June
Cauliflower	Feb. to April	$\frac{1}{2}$ in.	May to June	$2\frac{1}{2}$ ft.	2 ft.	July to Nov.
Beans, broad	Nov. & Feb. to April	2 in.		3 ft.	6 in.	June to Oct.
Beans, french	April to May	1 in.		2 to 3 ft.	6 in.	July to Oct.
Beans, runner	April to May	2 in.		5 ft.	9 to 12 in.	July to Oct.
Peas	March to June	$1\frac{1}{2}$ in.		2 to 5 ft.	3 to 4 in.	June to Oct.
Parsnip	March to April	1 in.		$1\frac{1}{2}$ ft.	9 in.	Sept. onwards
Carrots	March to July	$\frac{1}{4}$ in.		8 to 12 in.	4 to 8 in.	June onwards
Beetroot	April to July	1 in.		15 in.	6 to 8 in.	July to Oct.
Swede	May to June	$\frac{1}{2}$ in.		15 in.	9 in.	October onwards
Turnips	March to Sept.	$\frac{1}{2}$ in.		12 to 15 in.	6 to 8 in.	June onwards
Onions	March & Aug. to Sept.	$\frac{1}{2}$ in.	April	1 ft.	6 in.	June onwards
Leeks	March	$\frac{1}{4}$ in.	June	$1\frac{1}{2}$ ft.	9 in.	Sept. to May
Spinach, summer	March to July	1 in.		1 ft.	9 in.	May to Oct.
Spinach, winter	Aug. to Sept.	1 in.		1 ft.	4 in.	Oct. to April
Spinach beet	April to Aug.	1 in.		$1\frac{1}{2}$ ft.	9 in.	July onwards
Lettuce	March to Aug.	$\frac{1}{2}$ in.		1 ft.	9 to 12 in.	June to Oct.
Celery	Feb. to March	$\frac{1}{4}$ in.	May to June	3 ft.	1 ft.	Sept. to March

The Greenhouse

A greenhouse and some frames can contribute greatly to the enjoyment of a garden for they will extend the range of plants which can be grown and provide opportunities for plant propagation. A greenhouse equipped with all the modern aids will practically run itself and many of these are described in this chapter.

Although an unheated greenhouse can be of great use and interest, it is rather limited in its scope for frost cannot be excluded during the winter. Higher temperatures will be maintained if the greenhouse is lined with thin clear polythene sheeting to serve the same purpose as double glazing. I think that camellias are good plants for the unheated house for they can withstand quite a bit of frost and in a greenhouse they will start to flower in late January or February and continue into May or even June. Other shrubs which can be forced include evergreen azaleas, lilac and forsythia. I would also grow a selection of early-flowering bulbs – narcissi, irises and hyacinths – and for later flowering some hardy annuals – clarkia, cornflower, godetia and mignonette. For the summer there are many plants to choose from among which are some of my favourites – pelargoniums, gloxinias, fuchsias and begonias. Hardy lettuce varieties can be grown during the winter months and tomatoes during the summer.

A greenhouse heated to maintain a minimum winter temperature of 7°C. (45°F.) is termed a cool greenhouse and the range of plants which can be grown is extended. For the early months there are cinerarias, *Azalea indica* and *Primula obconica*. These can be followed by calceolarias and schizanthus. Later there are the achimenes, campanulas and lily species and for the winter forced bulbs, chrysanthemums, abutilons, primulas and *Solanum capsicastrum*, the winter cherry with its orange-red berries. Bedding plants and some vegetable seedlings can also be raised in a cool greenhouse.

The winter temperature in a warm greenhouse should never fall below 10°C. (50°F.) and should preferably be 13°C. (55°F.). However, the cost of heating a warm greenhouse can be almost double that of a cool greenhouse but for the enthusiast the list of plants which can be grown is almost endless. It includes lovely climbing plants, highly decorative foliage plants, orchids and ferns.

Siting The most important consideration when choosing a site for the greenhouse and frames is to aim at placing them near to the house so that they are easy to get to in bad weather and there will be no difficulty in providing them with electricity supplies should these be needed. They must stand in an open position with plenty of light and I find that it is convenient to have a paved or gravelled area close by on which pot plants can be stood in summer. Try to avoid placing them in a draughty site as cold winds can quickly lower the internal house temperatures.

A conservatory or sun lounge can also be a great source of pleasure. It must be south or west-facing and if connected by french windows to the living room it makes a pleasant place to sit on wet or windy days.

Types of greenhouse Modern greenhouses are made in aluminium, steel or wood. The traditional style is the span-roof house and this is really the most adaptable kind for the home gardener. The standard kind has low walls of brick or wood [1] with staging on both sides at the level where the glass starts but it is also possible to have it glazed to ground level [2].

For a more restricted site the three-quarter span or lean-to house is useful. Both these types make use of a house wall for one of their sides and this not only provides an area for training peaches or greenhouse climbers but also transfers some heat from the house. The three-quarter span has more glass area than the lean-to with the subsequent advantages of allowing more light to enter and having more provision for better ventilation. The lean-to is neat and space saving [3] and a good buy for the small garden. Both the three-quarter span and the lean-to should be placed against south or west-facing walls.

Frames At its simplest, a frame is a box covered with a sheet of glass known as a light. The traditional type with wooden sides and sliding lights is one of the most popular but frames may also have brick [4] or concrete walls and many are available now made of metal, plastic or fibreglass. They make a useful adjunct to a greenhouse, providing an area where plants can be hardened off a process of acclimatization which should always accompany the removal of any plant from an artificial to a natural climate. Hardening off is done by slowly increasing the ventilation in the frame by raising the lights gradually more

each day until they can be removed altogether.

Frames are also a good place in which to root cuttings and germinate seedlings. They become much more useful for this purpose if they are provided with some form of heating and one of the most convenient methods is with special electric warming cables [5]. These may be clipped around the sides of the frames or buried in sand about 4 to 6 in. below the soil surface. It is important that all electrical equipment used in frames is completely waterproof and I advise you to have it installed by an electrician.

Other ways of heating include the use of small oil heaters or hot water pipes. On cold nights loss of heat from the frames can be cut down by covering the lights with hessian or mats.

Cloches The most important use of cloches is for protecting early sowings, particularly those of vegetable crops. They can also be used to raise bedding plants, to protect the more delicate flowers from bad weather and to hasten the maturity of certain vegetables and fruits.

There are a number of types of cloche available, made in glass [6] or plastic.

A greenhouse can contribute greatly to the enjoyment of a garden for the range of plants
which can be grown is extended

GREENHOUSE ACCESSORIES

Staging When greenhouse plants are grown in pots it is usually most convenient to stand them on staging, which is simply platforms placed at about table height. Sometimes, if the layout of the greenhouse allows, the staging can be arranged in tiers [1] to allow for display and to make maximum use of the space available.

Staging may be either of open slat or solid construction. Open staging is usually made of wooden slats spaced about an inch apart [2]. It is easily portable. Solid staging can be made from cement, concrete or corrugated iron sheeting bases which are covered with a layer of sand, gravel or small stone chippings [3]. The open staging is generally more suitable for the plants which prefer a drier atmosphere while the solid staging retains more moisture and is better for plants requiring a lot of humidity. The open slat staging can be adapted for use with moisture-loving plants by covering it with a polythene sheet and then placing on this a layer of gravel [4].

Beds of soil at floor level should be at least 9 in. deep.

Pots Plastic, as a material for making pots, has now almost entirely superseded clay. Plastic pots are light in weight, less breakable, and easier to store and clean. Plants grown in plastic pots tend to dry out less quickly than in clay so great care is needed when watering them.

The most frequently used sizes are 3½ in., 5 in., 7 in. and 9 in. and these will cover all the plants usually grown. Seed trays for raising young plants are also available in plastic.

Composts I like to use the John Innes composts for seed sowing and potting. These are standardized compost mixtures which can either be bought ready mixed or prepared at home. The basic ingredients are soil, peat and sand and if you are going to make your own the soil should be sterilized by standing it over boiling water or placing it in one of the special sterilizers [5] available for this purpose. The temperature of the soil should be raised to 93°C. (200°F.) and kept at this level for 20 minutes.

The seed compost is made up of 2 parts by bulk of sterilized soil and 1 part each of peat and coarse sand. To each bushel of this mixture you will need to add 1½ oz. of superphosphate and ¾ oz. of ground limestone.

The potting composts are prepared from 7 parts by bulk of sterilized soil, 3 parts of peat and 2 parts of coarse sand. To this should be added a base fertilizer [6] which can be purchased ready mixed or made up from 2 parts by weight of hoof and horn meal, 2 parts of superphosphate and 1 part of sulphate of potash. This is added to the other ingredients at the rate of 4 oz. per bushel for No. 1 compost, 8 oz. per bushel for No. 2 and 12 oz. per bushel for No. 3. In addition, to No. 1 add ¾ oz. of ground chalk or limestone per bushel and double and treble this amount for Nos. 2 and 3. If the compost is intended for use with lime-hating plants the chalk or limestone should be omitted.

Many other proprietary composts based on peat are available and these can be used in place of the John Innes composts.

Heating Although quite a lot of plants can be grown in an unheated greenhouse, it cannot be used as a permanent house for tender plants unless frost can be excluded. If you can provide sufficient heat to keep the frost out in even the coldest weather, the range of plants which can be grown will be increased. And by maintaining a temperature of 7°C. (45°F.) the scope of the house can be further extended. But heating becomes a question of economics and the cost of providing the higher temperatures rises disproportionately.

Paraffin heaters For simplicity and cheapness nothing can beat a portable paraffin heater. Special models are made for the greenhouse which are fitted with water troughs to maintain a good level of humidity [1]. However, fumes can be a problem and such heaters must be kept very clean, never turned up too high and should have their wicks trimmed regularly.

Natural gas heaters Very useful portable heaters are now available which will burn natural gas and this has the added advantage that the by-products of combustion are carbon dioxide and water vapour, both of which are beneficial to plants.

Oil and gas-fired boilers These are used with metal hot water pipes to provide a system of heating by which the water is circulated by thermosyphon action. The boilers require very little attention [2] but it is important to place gas-fired boilers and flues in a position where the gas fumes will not be likely to get into the greenhouse. This does not apply to boilers fired by natural gas, as the fumes from this are harmless to plants.

The pipes used with this system are usually 4 in. in diameter and must be installed with a steady rise of about 1 in. in 10 ft. to their furthest point from the boiler with a corresponding fall on the return journey.

Solid-fuel boilers These can be used with the hot water pipe system but they require more attention than gas-fired ones [3].

Electrical heating This is the most adaptable method of heating for the greenhouse but it is also likely to be the most expensive. Tubular heaters provide an even distribution of heat and can be installed singly or in banks [4], the usual loading is 60 watts per foot run of tube. Fan-assisted heaters [5] can be used and these have the advantage of being portable. It is also possible to use an immersion heater in conjunction with the hot water pipe system.

Soil warming [6] is an especially valuable form of heating as it is used to provide bottom heating in propagating cases as well as in the greenhouse border. Two kinds of electrical soil warming are available: low voltage current reduced by a transformer can be passed through bare wires or current at full mains voltage can be passed through soil-warming cable. Both types should be buried 4 to 6 in. deep. It is important that all installation of electrical equipment should be carried out by a qualified electrician.

Controlling the temperature Temperature is of major importance to good plant cultivation and there are four things required in the greenhouse for accurate temperature regulation: thermostatic controls for the heating equipment, insulation, ventilation and shading.

Temperature control in winter depends largely on controlling the supply of artificial heat and much of the modern heating equipment can be thermostatically controlled. In fact, a thermostat is usually incorporated with electric and natural gas heaters as well as oil-fired boilers. If the heating apparatus is not equipped with them, separate thermostats can be used [1]. I also find a maximum-minimum thermometer [2] to be a valuable piece of equipment for monitoring temperatures.

Insulation can make a considerable difference to the heating bills. I find the simplest method is to fit polythene sheeting inside the roof glass, though it will be necessary to make provision for the opening of the ventilators [3]. With this method there will be some loss of light but whether it will be critical or not will depend on the sort of plants being grown. Any cracks in the house will allow for a great deal of

heat loss; these are most likely to occur in wooden houses and I pack all such cracks with glass wool, asbestos packing or any other suitable heat-insulation material.

Temperature control in summer depends mainly on ventilation and shading. Ventilation is necessary to change the air and keep the temperature from rising too high and it should be supplied even during the winter but draughts must be avoided. The most important ventilators are those near the ridge of the house and these should be positioned so that half are on one side and half on the other of a span-roof house. In this way they can be opened away from the prevailing wind. Ventilators in the sides of the house are useful to give a through current of air in very hot summer weather but they can cause draughts if not carefully used. The greenhouse door may also be left open to give additional ventilation. The aim should be to maintain a fairly even temperature but higher by day than at night.

Some form of automatic ventilation is a boon for the gardener who is away from home during the critical part of the day when the temperature reaches its highest point. Ventilators can be

automatically opened by a device which operates on a heat-sensitive fluid contained within a cylinder [4]. As the temperature rises, the fluid expands and pushes out a piston which opens the ventilator, as the temperature falls the converse happens and the ventilator is closed.

Extractor fans [5] can be thermostatically controlled to operate automatically. They should be powerful enough to change the air every three or four minutes.

Shading is also a means, when combined with ventilation, of preventing the air from becoming over-heated. Plants vary a lot in their need for shade and for this reason I think it is best to use a system of roller blinds [6] which can be easily raised or lowered. These blinds are usually made of fabric or polythene if they are used inside the house or of wooden lath or split cane if used outside. A cheaper alternative is to paint the glass with whitewash or one of the proprietary shading compounds. The most obvious disadvantage of this method of shading is that it is relatively permanent and is, therefore, a problem during dull spells, when it may greatly reduce the light available inside the greenhouse.

This summer border shows how attractive bedding plants can look when planted with imagination

Watering This is a skilful job as different plants need different amounts of water at different times of the year and it is impossible to generalize and give one rule which applies to everything. When watering seeds or young cuttings always use a coarse or fine rose on the watering-can [1]. All other plants should be watered from the spout and this should be held close to the pot [2] so that no soil is displaced and the water does not splash on the stems and leaves. Each time you water give sufficient to soak the soil right through and then do not give any more until it begins to dry out. With a bit of practice you will be able to decide when this stage is reached by examining or feeling the surface of the soil and by lifting the pots and feeling their weight. Dry soil is lighter than wet soil and you will soon gain experience in judging their relative weights. In spring and summer I examine the plants in my greenhouse daily, or even twice a day, to see which ones need water but in autumn and winter this only needs to be done every three or four days.

There are now various automatic or semi-automatic systems of watering available and one which has become popular is the capillary bench. This is essentially a simple device which depends on the plants' ability to absorb water by capillary attraction from a base of damp sand. The bench used for this must be quite level and covered with sheets of polythene or asbestos cement or the sand can be contained in plastic trays. About an inch of sand is required. The water is supplied by means of periodic trickle irrigation or by perforated piping laid in the sand and connected to a source of water such as a jar [3] or a tank fitted with a ball valve [4]. Plastic pots without drainage crocks are best for use on capillary benches as their bases are thin and the soil inside them can easily be brought into contact with the sand on the bench. Water each plant well after it has been placed in position to start the capillary action then each plant will simply take up water from the bench according to its needs.

Other watering systems use such devices as plastic pipes to deliver water to each pot, sprinkler units placed above the bench or rubber tubing fitted with drip nozzles [5].

Damping down For most plants it is important in hot or dry weather to increase the atmospheric moisture by splashing water over the paths [6] and under the staging. This is known as damping down and I usually do it with a watering-can fitted with a coarse rose. It also helps to spray the air, and the plants themselves if they are the kinds which enjoy such treatment. Morning and mid-day are the most suitable times.

Propagation I have dealt with seed sowing on page 51 and the taking of cuttings on pages 34 and 52 but I want to put in a word here about the greenhouse apparatus which makes propagation easier.

A propagating frame is one which is kept for the job of raising seedlings and rooting cuttings. It can be quite simply a wooden box supplied with a light and fitted with heating cables or it can be one of the more elaborate electrically operated propagators [1].

Mist-propagator Essentially this is a means of keeping the cuttings fresh without confining them to a frame or propagator. The free circulation of air and exposure to sunlight increases their rate of growth and under such a system half-ripe cuttings will root in as little as three weeks and the large-leaved evergreen shrubs [2], which are usually difficult to increase, will root fairly easily.

The mist propagation unit can be established in a corner of the greenhouse and the rooting medium is a bed of sand [3] which should be provided with soil warming cables or installed over hot water pipes or some other heating apparatus. The moisture is supplied by frequent fine sprays of water from the nozzle at the top of the stand pipe in the middle of the bench. The longer the bench the more of these units that will be required. The spray units can be automatically controlled by a time switch or an electronic 'leaf' which is sensitive to moisture. Various types of apparatus are available and they must be installed according to manufacturer's instructions.

The cuttings can either be inserted in trays which are placed on the sand [4], or they can be inserted direct into a bed of sand [5]. Cuttings which have been rooted under mist or in a heated propagator must be hardened off, first in the greenhouse and then in a cold frame, before they are planted out of doors.

Cleaning Every winter I try to find time to clean the greenhouse thoroughly. If possible, remove the plants before starting, then wash down the glass both inside and outside using a long-handled broom, warm water and detergent [6]. The dirt which accumulates between the overlap of the glass can be removed with a thin strip of metal [7]. The woodwork and walls should be scrubbed with warm water containing some disinfectant to dislodge any pests.

Fumigation In the greenhouse, many of the pests and diseases can most easily be controlled by fumigation and for this purpose there are special smoke generators [8].

Index